# 101 CHAMPIONSHIP BASEBALL DRILLS

**Glenn Cecchini**
**Raissa Cecchini**
**Jeff Walker**

COACHES CHOICE™

ISBN: 1-57167-361-x
Library of Congress Catalog Card Number: 98-88944

Cover Design: Matthew Edwards
Cover Photos: Courtesy of David Gonzales
Production Manager: Michelle A. Summers

Coaches Choice Books is a division of:    Sagamore Publishing, Inc.
P.O. Box 647
Champaign, IL 61824-0647
Web Site: http//www.sagamorepub.com

# DEDICATION

*To our wonderful boys, Garin Cecchini and Gavin Cecchini. You have brought such laughter and joy into our lives. We are so proud of you and so thankful that God sent you to us. You are our blessing and our fulfillment. Thanks for being your own little selves.*

G.C. and R.C.

*To my big brother, Johnny Walker, the most talented individual I have ever known. Thank you for helping me to finally get my greatest gift of all, Gabriel.*

J.W.

# ACKNOWLEDGMENTS

We acknowledge the assistance of some very special individuals who have not only inspired us, but have also touched our lives:

- Our parents, Dick Cecchini and Trenie Cecchini, and Genevieve Prince and the late Dr. R.E. Prince, Jr. Thank you for your unconditional love, support, and encouragement to follow our dreams.

- The 1998 Barbe Buc Baseball seniors who posed for pictures in this book: Brent Carbo; Jared Gothreaux; Edward Guth; Craig Martel; Chan Mayard; and Neil Simoneaux.

- Chris Bruchhaus and Joe Lawrence for their help and knowledge with the drills and photography. Your friendship is deeply treasured.

- Steve Whitfield, for his photography skills and patience while shooting the drills for this book.

- Leon McGraw, area scout for the Philadelphia Phillies, whose wonderful personality and intelligence is always greatly appreciated.

- René Gayo, area scout for the Cleveland Indians, whose knowledge of the game of baseball is extraordinary. It is always going to be an all-night talk about baseball when we get together.

- Rick Jones from Tulane University, one of the brightest minds in college baseball.

- The many college coaches who have taken the time to share their knowledge of the game with us.

- Every athlete whom we have ever coached for committing themselves to excellence and making the Barbe High School baseball team a nationally ranked championship program.

*Glenn and Raissa Cecchini*

Thanks to the following individuals for demonstrating the qualities so desperately needed in the educators of the future: Huey P. Kinchen; Tom Purifoy; Bobby Reyes; James Richardson; Huberto Saenz; and Larry Woolley. And thanks to H.L. Polk Jr.—for being the model that all coaches should emulate.

*Jeff Walker*

# CONTENTS

# PREFACE

We wrote this book to provide baseball coaches at all competitive levels with a tool that will enable them to enhance the skills and attributes of their players. As a vehicle for teaching and learning, properly designed drills have been shown to have extraordinary value. *101 Championship Baseball Drills* features drills that we have collected, field-tested, and effectively utilized over the course of our careers in coaching.

The variety and applications of the various drills presented in this book have been designed to make learning both enjoyable and meaningful for the athlete. Coaches should select those drills that are appropriate to the existing skill level of their players and should make sure that their athletes adequately master the objectives in the drills chosen before advancing to more complex or more challenging drills.

As coaches who have long recognized the value of drills in the "teaching process" and have utilized a wide variety of drills to maximize the "on-the-field" potential of the athlete whom we've had the opportunity to coach, writing this book was an enriching experience. If in the process of using the drills in this book, coaches are better able to have a positive impact on the skill levels of their athletes, then the effort to author this book with have been a worthwhile endeavor.

*G.C.*
*R.C.*

# CHAPTER 1

# DRILLS FOR INFIELDERS

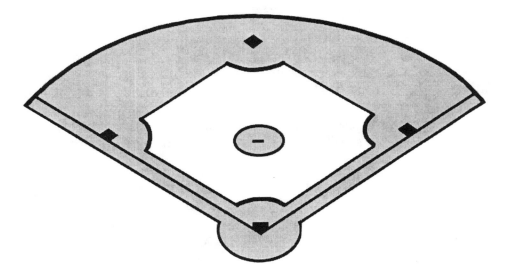

## DRILL #1: TRIANGLE FIELDING DRILL

*Objective:* To develop and sharpen the infielder's technique of fielding the three most common types of ground balls hit toward his position.

*Equipment Needed:* Three baseballs.

*Location:* Anywhere on the field.

*Description:* Three locations exist at which a ground ball may be hit toward an infielder; directly at him, to his backhand side, or to his glove side. The drill begins with an infielder standing in the ready position. The right-handed infielder should place his left foot slightly forward of the right foot while he keeps his feet shoulder width apart. Three balls are placed on the ground in front of the player. One baseball is placed 10 to 15 feet directly in front of him. A second baseball is placed 10 to 15 feet to his right, and a third baseball is placed 10 to 15 feet to his left. On the coach's command, the infielder should step with his right foot and move to field the ball that is directly in front of him (position #1). He should round the ball as he simulates fielding the ball hit directly at him. Rounding his path toward the ball hit directly at him allows the infielder to continue moving in the direction of his subsequent throw to first base. After completing the simulated fielding of the ball that is placed directly in front of him, the infielder should dropstep with his right foot and pivot to his right to field the ball originally placed to his right in position #2. When fielding the baseball that is placed in position #2, the infielder is practicing his backhand fielding technique. To simulate the backhand fielding technique, the infielder should place his right foot to the right of the ball and keep his left foot rearward.

The infielder should squat low while rotating the elbow of the glove-hand outward. He should then simulate the backhand of the ball in position #2 and fake the throw to first base. After faking the throw to first base, the infielder should open his hips to the left and pivot toward the ball located in position #3. He should then move to simulate the fielding of the ball, taking care to again round his path toward the baseball. He places his left foot to the inside of the ball as he simulates scooping the ball. He should form the letter "C" as he brings the glove to his chest and cocks the shoulders to throw the ball. Forming the "C" helps the player get his feet and body around before he simulates the throw to first base.

*Coaching Points:*

- The player should not touch the baseballs.
- In the early stages of practice, the drill should be first performed as a "walk-through."
- When simulating the fielding of the ball in position #2, the player should avoid "picking" at the ball. He must "pull" through it.
- When simulating the fielding of the ball in any of the three positions, the player should keep the midline of his body to the right of the ball, fielding the ball from his left side.
- A proper ready position involves having a player's weight on the balls of his feet. He should be able to throw in any direction.

**Drill #1: Triangle Drill—Field first ball; routine ground ball.**
***Emphasis Point: The player should concentrate on the ball he is fielding. Hypothetically, the first ball is a routine ground ball.***

## DRILL #2: TWO BALL DRILL

*Objective:* To improve the player's hand-eye coordination and foot coordination.

*Equipment Needed:* Five baseballs for each pair of players.

*Location:* Anywhere on the field.

*Description:* The players are randomly paired. Each player stacks two balls in his glove-hand, which is bare-handed. The two players stand approximately 10 feet apart as they face each other and play catch with the fifth ball. Each player uses the two balls stacked in his glove-hand for a glove. As the ball is tossed over-handed, the player who is catching the ball should turn his body slightly away from the player who is tossing the ball. Turning away from the player who is throwing the ball keeps the receiver's glove-hand near the thrower. This position places the body in the correct position to throw the ball once the player makes the catch. During this drill, the players should exhibit "happy feet" (i.e., feet continually moving in place in a short choppy manner).

*Coaching Points:*

- As the player catches the ball, he should visualize his arms as shock absorbers, relaxing his hands and elbows.
- The player should quickly catch and release the ball.
- This drill may be done with a glove on the glove-hand.
- The catcher should always provide a target for the thrower's toss.

**Drill #2: Two Ball Drill. *Emphasis point: The player should catch thrown ball off of the two balls in his glove hand.***

### DRILL #3: DEAD-AHEAD FRONT END DRILL

*Objective:* To teach the middle infielder the correct technique of turning a double play when the ball is hit directly at him.

*Equipment Needed:* A crate of baseballs; a base.

*Location:* In the infield near second base.

*Description:* A middle infielder waits in the ready position just prior to a feeder rolling the ball directly at him. Once the ball is released, the infielder charges the ball. As he closes to the ball, he should lower his body and set himself to catch the ball. After securing the ball, the infielder should open his hip closest to second base and side-arm throw the ball to the man covering the bag. The shortstop should field the ball with the second baseman covering the bag and practicing his double-play footwork. When the second baseman is fielding the ball, the shortstop should cover the bag and practice his double play footwork.

*Coaching Points:*

- The feeder should be positioned on the infield grass.
- The feeder should throw the ball with a $^3/_4$ arm-angle of motion. This makes the ball hop and better simulates an infield ground ball.
- The infielders should execute this drill from normal double-play positioning (i.e., closer to the infield grass and to second base).

**Drill #3: Dead-Ahead Front End Drill.**
*Emphasis point: The shortstop should open up his hips to make a throw to second.*

## DRILL #4: SHORT TO SECOND DRILL

*Objective:* To teach the second baseman the techniques of the backend receiver on the double play.

*Equipment Needed:* A crate of baseballs; a base.

*Location:* In the infield near second base.

*Description:* A feeder kneels on the ground or sits on a crate to toss the ball to the backend receiver. He should be in a position corresponding to that of a shortstop in the double play position who has just fielded a ball hit directly at him. The feeder tosses the ball to second base with a side-arm delivery . The second baseman should catch the ball as he executes the proper footwork for the double play—his left foot touches the bag, his right foot steps backward in the dirt, his left foot is in the dirt on the rightfield side of second base. The second baseman should hold his hands open at chest level, forming a "W" with his palms facing the ball and his fingers pointing to the sky. After receiving the throw from the shortstop, the second baseman should then simulate the throw to first base and hop over an imaginary player who is sliding into second base.

*Coaching Points:*

- The second baseman should receive the throw at the back point of second base.
- The second baseman should exhibit "happy feet" (i.e., feet continually moving in place in a short choppy manner), as he receives the throw and completes the double play.
- When the ball hits his glove, the second baseman should use the middle finger of his glove-hand to push the ball out of the glove. This step results in the ball quickly popping out to the throwing hand.
- The second baseman should catch the ball close to his chest—not out in front of him. This action allows him to turn the double play faster.
- The second baseman's throwing hand should always be held in a position to catch the ball once it is forced out of his glove.

## DRILL #5: SECOND TO SHORT DRILL

*Objective:* To teach the shortstop the techniques of the backend receiver on the double play.

*Equipment Needed:* A crate of baseballs; a base.

*Location:* In the infield near second base.

*Description:* A feeder kneels on the ground or sits on a crate to toss the ball to the backend receiver. He should be in a position corresponding to that of a second baseman in the double-play position who has just fielded a ball hit directly at him. The feeder should toss the ball to second base with a side-arm delivery . The shortstop should move to straddle the rear of second base, timing his movement so that his right foot drags across the back point of the base just as he receives the ball. Staying to the back of the base allows the shortstop to turn his body and get in the proper position to make the throw to first base. The shortstop's hands should be held at chest level, forming a "W" with his palms facing the ball and his fingers pointing to the sky. After receiving the toss and dragging his foot across the back point of the base, the shortstop should simulate the throw to first base as he hops over an imaginary player who is sliding into second base.

*Coaching Points:*

- The backend receiver should exhibit "happy feet" (i.e., feet continually moving in place in a short choppy manner) as he receives the throw and completes the double play.
- When the ball hits his glove, the backend receiver should use the middle finger of his glove-hand to push the ball out of the glove. This step results in the ball quickly popping out to the throwing hand.
- The second baseman's throwing hand should always be held in a position to catch the ball once it is forced out of his glove.

**DRILL #6: UNDERHAND FEED DRILL**

*Objective:* To teach the middle infielder how to underhand feed the ball to the backend receiver on the double play.

*Equipment Needed:* A crate of baseballs; a base.

*Location:* In the infield around second base.

*Description:* The feeder should kneel on the ground or sit on a crate in the infield grass. The infielder who will be the frontend of the double play should assume the ready position and await the toss of the ball. The feeder rolls the ball between the base and the frontend infielder. The infielder should sprint toward the ball and field the ball on the move. The fielder should clearly present the ball to the backend receiver by immediately pulling his glove away from the ball as he begins to make the feed. He should then use an underhand motion to toss the ball to the backend receiver at second base.

*Coaching Points:*

- The frontend fielder should actually put his glove behind his back as he makes the underhand feed.
- The frontend fielder should grasp the ball in a manner so that the ball is held firmly between the second and third knuckle of each finger.
- The frontend fielder should keep a "stiff wrist" when performing the underhand feed.
- The right-handed fielder should use his left foot to step toward the backend receiver, following through with his right foot.

**Drill #6: Underhand Feed Drill.** *Emphasis point: The second baseman should feed the ball to the shortstop.*

14

## DRILL #7: FRONT END-BACKHAND DRILL

*Objective:* To teach the technique of fielding using the backhand and turning a double play.

*Equipment Needed:* A crate of baseballs; a base.

*Location:* In the infield around second base.

*Description:* The feeder should kneel on the ground or sit on a crate in the infield grass. The infielder who will be the frontend of the double play should assume the ready position and await the toss of the ball. The feeder rolls the ball to the infielder's backhand. The infielder should react by sprinting toward the ball and breaking down. When fielding the ball, the right-handed infielder should plant his right foot on the right side of the ball, keeping the ball at his midline. He should bend his knees and squat down to catch the ball, making sure that his left leg is back. After catching the ball, the frontend fielder should open the left knee and rotate his hips to throw the ball to second base.

*Coaching Points:*

- When fielding the ball, the right-handed player's left knee should almost touch the ground.
- The fielder should rotate the elbow of his glove-hand outward and pull through the ball as he makes the catch.
- The fielder should make a strong side arm throw to second.
- The fielder should stay low on the throw.

**Drill #7: Front End-Backhand Drill.** *Emphasis Point: The fielder should lower himself to the ground.*

## DRILL #8: WORM AND TURN DRILL

*Objective:* To teach the second baseman the footwork needed for turning a double play when the ball is hit deep in the hole to the shortstop.

*Equipment Needed:* A crate of baseballs; a base.

*Location:* In the infield around second base.

*Description:* A feeder throws the ball in the hole between the shortstop and second base using a $3/4$-arm angle of motion. The shortstop should move to field the ball and makes the throw to second base. The second baseman should move to cover second base, timing his arrival at second base so that he gets to the base at the same moment the ball arrives on the throw from the shortstop. The second baseman should turn the double play using the proper sequence of footwork—his left foot touches the bag, his right foot steps backward in the dirt, his left foot is in the dirt on the rightfield side of second base. The second baseman should hold his hands open at chest level, forming a "W" with his palms facing the ball and his fingers pointing to the sky. The second baseman should receive the throw at the back point of the base. After receiving the throw from the shortstop, the second baseman should then simulate the throw to first base and hop over an imaginary player who is sliding into second base.

*Coaching Points:*

- The second baseman should exhibit "happy feet" (i.e., feet continually moving in place in a short choppy manner), as he receives the throw and completes the double play.
- When the ball hits his glove, the second baseman should use the middle finger of his glove-hand to push the ball out of his glove. This step results in the ball quickly popping out to the throwing hand.
- The second baseman's throwing hand should always be held in a position to catch the ball once it is forced out of the glove.
- When completing the footwork of the double play, the second baseman should point his left foot toward first base to open his hips.

**Drill #8: Worm and Turn Drill.**
*Emphasis point: The second baseman should put himself into the proper position to receive the throw from the shortstop.*

## DRILL #9: SECOND WORM AND TURN DRILL

*Objective:* To teach the second baseman how to field the ball hit deep in the hole towards first base and turn a double play.

*Equipment Needed:* A crate of baseballs; a base.

*Location:* In the infield around second base.

*Description:* A feeder throws the ball in the hole between second base and shortstop using a $3/4$ arm angle of motion. The feeder aims his toss so that it hits a short distance from the second baseman's glove hand. The second baseman should sprint to field the ball. Once he catches the ball, the second baseman should complete the double play by exercising one of three options.

- Dropstep with his right foot, open his hip, and throw the ball to the shortstop at second base.
- Spin to the right (i.e., clockwise) and throw the ball to the shortstop at second base.
- Spin to the left (i.e., counter-clockwise) and throw the ball to the shortstop at second base.

*Coaching Points:*

- The second baseman should be well-practiced at the three available options on making the throw to the shortstop at second base.
- The second baseman must not hesitate when executing one of the three options.
- The second baseman should stay low and quickly make a strong throw to the base.
- The shortstop should execute the correct technique of the backend receiver as described the Backend to the Shortstop Drill (Drill #5).
- This drill, like Drill #1, could be broken into three parts.

**Drill #9: Second Worm and Turn Drill.**
*Emphasis point: The second baseman should employ the proper techniques when making a throw on the front end of a double play ball.*

## DRILL #10: SOFT HANDS STILL DRILL

*Objective:* To teach the infielders to have "soft hands" when handling the baseball.

*Equipment Needed:* A crate of baseballs.

*Location:* Anywhere.

*Description:* No glove is needed for this drill. Two players face each other a short distance apart. The feeder kneels down or sits on a crate. The feeder throws the ball in such a manner as to make the ball hop, simulating a ground ball hit to the infielder. The right-handed infielder assumes the ready position and awaits the throw, keeping his left foot slightly in front of the right. The ball is tossed straight at the infielder so that the infielder doesn't have to move laterally. When fielding the ball, the infielder should position his body so that his midline is to the right of the ball. The infielder should use the funnel technique on regular ground balls and the push-through technique on short hop ground balls. The funnel technique involves the infielder cushioning the impact of the ball as it hits the hands. The push-through technique involves the infielder catching the ball by pushing his glove forward through the ball as he points the fingers downward.

*Coaching Points:*

- The infielder should keep his head down when fielding the ball.
- The infielder should keep his hands out in front of his feet.
- The coach should check to make sure that the infielder brings the ball up to the midline after catching the ball.
- The infielder should keep the fingers of his glove-hand pointed downward.
- The infielder should stay low when fielding the ball.

**Drill #10: Soft Hands Still Drill.**

## DRILL #11: SOFT HANDS STILL DRILL—BACKHAND

*Objective:* To teach the infielders to have "soft hands" when handling the baseball that is hit to his backhand.

*Equipment Needed:* A crate of baseballs.

*Location:* Anywhere.

*Description:* No glove is needed for this drill. Two players face each other a short distance apart. One player throws the ball in such a manner as to make the ball hop, simulating a ground ball hit to the infielder. The ball is tossed toward the backhand side of the infielder. The infielder should field the ball without moving laterally. The infielder should turn his body sideways and keep his left leg back as he bends his knees. The infielder should use the pull-through technique on short hop ground balls. The pull-through technique involves the infielder catching the ball by pulling through the ball as he points the fingers downward, as his elbow is rotated out and upward.

*Coaching Points:*

- The infielder should keep his head down when fielding the ball.
- The infielder should keep the elbow of his glove-hand pointed outward and upward.
- The coach should check to make sure that the infielder brings the ball to his midline after fielding the ball.
- The infielder should keep the fingers of his glove-hand pointed downward.
- The infielder should stay low when fielding the ball.

## DRILL #12: PADDLE DRILL

*Objective:* To develop an infielder's hand-eye coordination.

*Equipment Needed:* A crate of baseballs; foam paddles.

*Location:* Anywhere.

*Description:* Two players face each other a short distance apart. One player throws the ball in such a manner as to make the ball hop, simulating a ground ball hit to the infielder. The right-handed infielder assumes the ready position and awaits the throw, keeping his left foot slightly in front of the right. The ball is tossed directly toward the infielder who is holding a foam paddle in each hand. The infielder should use the funnel technique on regular ground balls and the push-through technique on short hop ground balls. The funnel technique involves the infielder cushioning the impact of the ball as it hits the hands. The push-through technique involves the infielder catching the ball by pushing his glove forward through the ball as he points the fingers downward.

*Coaching Points:*

- The coaching points are identical as for Drill #10 (the Soft Hands Still Drill).
- The players should strive to make the catch without making any noise.
- The drill may be run with a feeder hitting fungos to the infielder from the mound.

**Drill #12: Paddle Drill.**

## DRILL #13: CHAIR DRILL

*Objective:* To train the fielder to stay low and allow him the opportunity to experience the feeling from the correct lower body position when fielding a ground ball.

*Equipment Needed:* A crate of baseballs; a folding chair; foam paddles.

*Location:* Anywhere.

*Description:* Two players face each other a short distance apart. The fielder sits on the front edge of the chair's seat. The right-handed fielder should position his feet with the left foot slightly in front of the right. The feeder should toss ground balls to the glove side of the fielder, straight at the fielder, and to the fielder's backhand. The fielder can use a glove, a paddle, or his barehand.

*Coaching Points:*

- The ball cannot be backhanded when the fielder is using paddles.
- The coach should check to make sure that the fielder is sitting on the edge of the chair.
- The fielder should keep his head down, his eyes on the baseball, and his elbows slightly bent.

**Drill #13: Chair Drill. *Emphasis Point: The fielder should sit on the edge of the chair.***

## DRILL #14: Z-BALL DRILL

*Objective:* To improve the player's hand-eye and foot coordination.

*Equipment Needed:* A Z-Ball (a jack-shaped high energy rubber ball).

*Location:* Anywhere.

*Description:* Two players stand approximately fifteen to twenty feet apart facing each other. On the coach's command, they should chop their feet in place, keeping their weight on the balls of their feet (i.e., exhibit happy feet). The players should continue to exhibit happy feet as they throw the Z-Ball back and forth to each other so that it bounces.

*Coaching Point:*

- The fielder should keep his head down, his eyes on the Z-Ball, and his elbows slightly bent.

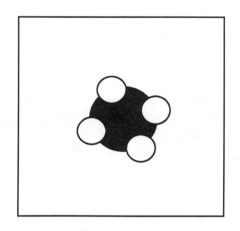

**Drill #14: Z-Ball Drill.**

## DRILL #15: BAREHAND GROUND BALL DRILL

*Objective:* To improve the infielder's "soft hands" technique when handling the baseball.

*Equipment Needed:* A crate of baseballs; a batting glove; a fungo bat.

*Location:* Infield.

*Description:* An infielder wearing a batting glove on his glove-hand positions himself on the infield dirt. A feeder initially positions himself midway between home plate and the infielder. The feeder uses a fungo bat to hit routine ground balls directly to the infielder. After the infielder has demonstrated proficiency at fielding the routine grounders, the feeder should vary the direction and speed of the ball. The drill continues as the infielders finishes the play by rolling the ball back to the feeder. As the drill proceeds, the feeder should move to home plate and should hit the ball harder.

*Coaching Points:*

- The infielder should keep his head down when fielding the ball.
- The infielder should demonstrate "happy feet" when fielding the ball.
- The players may opt to not use the batting glove.
- The drill should incorporate all types of ground balls—routine, bounders, backhands, and forehands.

**Drill 15: Barehand Ground Ball Drill.**

## MOVEMENT AND SPECIALTY DRILLS

### DRILL #16: MIRROR DRILL

*Objective:* To increase the player's stamina.

*Equipment Needed:* Two baseballs for each pair of players.

*Location:* Anywhere.

*Description:* Two baseballs are placed on the ground approximately fifteen feet apart. A pair of players face each other as they stand on opposite sides of one of the baseballs. On the coach's command, both players assume the ready position. The players should then slide from the first ball to the second ball. When the players reach the second ball, they should pretend to field the ball, then retrace their path back to their starting point (i.e., the first ball). Both players should continue the drill for a specified number of repetitions or until the coach signals the end of their turn.

*Coaching Points:*

- The players should slide from ball to ball without crossing their feet.
- The players should stay low.
- The players should practice the various types of fielding situations—backhand, forehand, and routine ground balls.

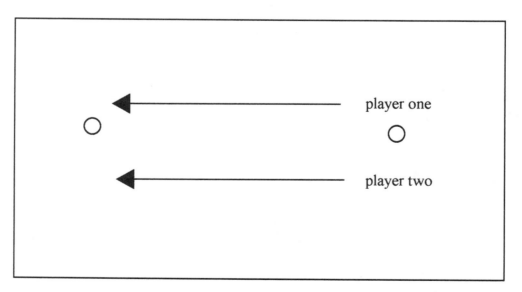

**Drill #16: Mirror Drill.**

## DRILL #17: DIVE DRILL

*Objective:* To teach the infielder the fundamentals of finishing a play after diving to catch the ball.

*Equipment Needed:* A glove; a baseball.

*Location:* Infield dirt.

*Description:* The infielder places a baseball in his glove and assumes the ready position. The coach points in one direction. The infielder should react by turning his body toward the direction in which the coach pointed and diving to the ground. The infielder's belly should contact the ground. Using his elbows and knees to push upward, the infielder should then return to his feet and regain an athletic position in order to throw the ball.

*Coaching Points:*

- The drill should involve the fielding techniques for various types of ground balls—forehand, backhand, and regular.
- The drill may be extended by having the player throw the ball to a specific location after returning to the throwing position.

## DRILL #18: TAG DRILL

*Objective:* To teach the infielder how to apply a tag to a player who is sliding into a base.

*Equipment Needed:* Crate of baseballs; a base; a glove.

*Location:* Near any base.

*Description:* The infielder works at a position around a familiar base (e.g., the first baseman works near first base, the second baseman works near second base, etc.). A feeder kneels approximately thirty feet from the infielder. The feeder begins the drill by throwing the ball towards the infielder covering the base. The infielder who is covering the base should catch the ball and simulate a tag on an imaginary baserunner sliding into the base.

*Coaching Points:*

• The infielder should make quick tags.
• The infielder should squeeze the ball with his glove, ensuring that the ball will not be knocked free from his glove-hand.

**Drill #18: Tag Drill.** *Emphasis point: The fielder should straddle the bag and give the imaginary baserunner a firm quick tag.*

## DRILL #19: BOUNDER DRILL

*Objective:* To improve the infielder's ability to catch a baseball that is hit hard into the ground and is bouncing slowly toward him.

*Equipment Needed:* Crate of baseballs; a fungo bat; a glove.

*Location:* Infield.

*Description:* The infielders assume their positions and ready themselves for play. The feeder uses a fungo bat to hit a slow, choppy ground ball toward a specific infielder. The fielding player should round his path to the ball so that his momentum is toward the direction in which he is throwing. The right-handed fielder should field the ball on the left of his midline. After fielding the ball, the player should take an additional step with his right foot and simulate a throw to first base. When fielding a ball hit to the left of his midline, the right-handed player should make sure that the ball is fielded just outside his left foot. When using his barehand to field the ball, the player should make sure that the ball is fielded just outside his right foot and throw on the run.

*Coaching Points:*

- This drill may be initiated with the feeder throwing the ball to the infielder.
- The infielder should attempt to field all bounders with his glove-hand, unless the situation demands extraordinary speed in securing the ball and delivering it to the specified base.

**Drill #19: Bounder Drill. *Emphasis point: The fielder should catch the ball off his outside left foot and throw off his right foot.***

## DRILL #20: DEAD BALL DRILL

*Objective:* To improve the infielder's ability in fielding a dead ball.

*Equipment Needed:* A crate of baseballs.

*Location:* Infield grass.

*Description:* The infielder assumes the ready position for play. The ball is placed on the grass in front of the fielder. On the coach's command, the infielder should sprint to the ball and break down to field the ball. The fielding player should round his path to the ball so that his momentum is toward the direction in which he is throwing. To barehand field the ball, a right-handed fielder should field the ball just outside of his right foot. After barehand fielding the ball, the player should take an additional step with his left foot and throw the ball to first base.

*Coaching Points:*

- The infielder should use all of his hand to field the ball, not just his fingers.
- The infielder should quickly throw the ball to first base.

## DRILL #21: FOUL BALL DRILL

*Objective:* To improve the infielder's decision-making skills on fielding the ball that is hit down the line.

*Equipment Needed:* A crate of baseballs; a glove

*Location:* Infield near the foul lines.

*Description:* The infielder assumes the ready position for play. A feeder rolls the ball down one of the foul lines. The infielder should sprint to the ball, reading the spin of the ball and the angle of the ball's path down the line. If he determines that the ball is going to be foul, the infielder should act appropriately (i.e., let it go foul). Once the ball is actually in foul territory, the infielder should position himself in foul territory and sweep up the ball so that the umpire calls the ball foul.

*Coaching Point:*

- The feeder should roll the ball as close to the line as possible.

## DRILL #22: INFIELD POP-UP DRILL

*Objective:* To teach the infielder how to position himself to catch an infield pop-up.

*Equipment Needed:* A crate of baseballs; a glove; a pitching machine.

*Location:* Baseball field.

*Description:* The coach sets up a pitching machine so that it will send pop-up fly balls into the air. The infielders go to their positions and assume the ready position. When the machine shoots a pop-up into the air, the infielders move toward a position under the ball. The infielder who is in the best position to catch the pop-up should yell "ball, ball, ball" continuously. The infielder yells "ball" until he hears "take it, take it" from a teammate. The infielders who are not fielding the ball should move away from the fielder so that they do not interfere with his catch.

*Coaching Points:*

- The feeder should shoot balls to various locations throughout the infield, including foul territory.
- If a coach doesn't have a pitching machine, he can hit tennis balls with a fungo bat. Tennis balls are easy to handle, can be hit fairly high, and tend to move about in flight.

## DRILL #23: RELAY DRILL

*Objective:* To teach the infielder how to position himself to receive a throw from an outfielder that needs to be relayed to a teammate.

*Equipment Needed:* One baseball for each group.

*Location:* Anywhere.

*Description:* Five players stand approximately 15 yards apart in a line. The player at one end begins the drill by throwing the ball to the closest player. The player who is receiving the throw should turn his body so that his glove-hand is away from the thrower. The receiver should use two hands to catch the ball and quickly should throw the ball to the next player in line. The ball should continue to be relayed down the line to the last player. The last player should catch the ball and spin in a direction opposite his throwing arm, and reverse the direction of the ball by throwing it to his closest teammate.

*Coaching Points:*

- The players should throw the ball to a point between the chest and head of the receiver.
- When receiving the throw, the players should form a "W" with their hands. Forming a "W" allows a receiver to quickly get the ball out of the glove.
- The coach should check to make sure that the players turn sideways when receiving the throw.

### DRILL #24: HALF DISTANCE FUNGO DRILL

*Objective:* To improve the infielder's reaction as he fields a ground ball.

*Equipment Needed:* A crate of baseballs; a fungo bat.

*Location:* Infield.

*Description:* A feeder hits fungo from designated midway points. When hitting to the middle infielder, the feeder should hit fungo from a point in the dirt directly in front of the mound. When hitting to the third baseman, the feeder hits fungo from a point midway between home plate and third base. When hitting to the first baseman, the feeder should hit fungo from a point midway between home plate and first base.

*Coaching Point:*

•    The infielder may make the throw to first base or simulate the throw to first base and roll the ball back to the fungo hitter.

## DRILL #25: RAPID FIRE DRILL

*Objective:* To improve the infielder's hand-eye coordination.

*Equipment Needed:* A crate of baseballs; a paddle.

*Location:* Infield.

*Description:* A feeder throws short hops to an infielder who is using a paddle on his glove-hand. The hops should be delivered so that the throws arrive at the infielder's position in rapid succession. The feeder counts how many balls that the infielder catches without committing an error. After one player completes a round of fielding, the players should switch roles.

*Coaching Points:*

- The feeder should throw the balls in rapid succession.
- After catching the ball, the infielder should quickly toss the ball away without taking his eyes off of the feeder.
- The coach should check to make sure that the fielder demonstrates the proper fundamentals for fielding a ground ball.

## DRILL #26: CIRCLE TAPS DRILL

*Objective:* To improve the infielder's hand-eye coordination and concentration on the ball.

*Equipment Needed:* One baseball.

*Location:* Anywhere.

*Description:* Approximately six to eight players form a circle. On the command of the coach, they assume an athletic stance. A player starts the drill by rolling the ball to any player. The player to whom the ball is rolled may use either hand to push the ball to a third player. The ball is rolled from player to player. If a player misses the ball, he must exit the circle. The drill should continue until only one player is left.

*Coaching Points:*

- The coach should emphasize to the players to stay low and keep their hands out in front of their body.
- The players should not stop the ball; instead, they should keep the ball moving by pushing the ball with their fingers.
- Younger players should use a rag ball during this drill for an increased level of safety.

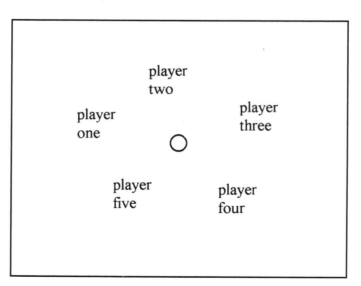

**Drill #26: Circle Taps Drill.**

## DRILL #27: AROUND THE HORN DRILL

*Objective:* To improve the infielder's quickness and agility

*Equipment Needed:* One baseball.

*Location:* An infield.

*Description:* A catcher, a third baseman, a second baseman, and a first baseman take their positions in the infield, straddling their respective base. The catcher initiates the drill by throwing the ball to the third baseman. The third baseman should receive the throw from the catcher and throws the ball to the second baseman. The second baseman should receive the throw from the third baseman and throw the ball to the first baseman. The first baseman should receive the ball from the third baseman and complete the circuit by throwing the ball to the catcher.

*Coaching Points:*

- All the throws should be made in a clockwise circuit.
- Each player should throw the ball to a point on the receiver's body between the receiver's chest and head.
- Each fielder should hold his hands in the "W" position to catch the throw.
- Each fielder should exhibit happy feet as he glides toward the thrown ball.
- Each fielder should step toward the receiving teammate as he throws the ball.

## DRILL #28: JUMP TURN AROUND THE HORN DRILL

*Objective:* To improve the infielder's ability to execute the jump-turn maneuver.

*Equipment Needed:* One baseball; a glove.

*Location:* An infield.

*Description:* A catcher, a first baseman, a shortstop and a third baseman take their positions in the infield, straddling their respective base. The catcher initiates the drill by throwing the ball to the first baseman. The first baseman should receive the throw from the catcher and throw the ball to the shortstop. The shortstop—who is covering second base—should receive the throw from the first baseman and throw the ball to the third baseman. The third baseman should receive the ball from the shortstop and complete the circuit by throwing the ball to the catcher. Each fielder should execute the jump-turn maneuver after receiving a throw. To execute a jump-turn maneuver, the right-handed infielder's right foot should replace his left foot. The right-handed infielder completes a jump-turn maneuver by using his left foot to step toward the receiver as he throws the ball.

*Coaching Points:*

- All the throws should be made in a counter-clockwise circuit.
- Each player should throw the ball to a point on the receiver's body between the receiver's chest and head.
- On a jump-turn, the receiving player should turn towards the outfield.
- Each fielder should hold his hands in the "W" position to catch the throw.
- Each fielder should exhibit happy feet as he glides toward the thrown ball.
- Each fielder should step to the toward the receiving teammate as he throws the ball.

## DRILL #29: CATCH—EXPLODE—THROW—GROUND BALL DRILL

*Objective:* To develop the infielder's use of the proper techniques of catching and throwing the ball.

*Equipment Needed:* A crate of baseballs; a glove.

*Location:* Anywhere.

*Description:* The fielder faces a feeder who is standing or sitting approximately 25 feet away from him. The fielder should demonstrate an athletic stance as he assumes the ready position. The right-handed fielder should stagger his left foot slightly ahead of his right foot. The feeder throws a regular ground ball to the fielder. The fielder should freeze after securing the ball on the catch so that the coach can check his technique markers. After checking the fielder's technique markers in catching the ball, the coach gives the "explode" command. The fielder should respond to the coach's command by moving into the correct throwing position and then pausing. The coach should then check the fielder's throwing-position technique markers. After checking the fielder's technique markers in his movement to the throwing position, the coach gives the "throw" command. The fielder should respond to the coach's command to throw by throwing the ball to the feeder and freezing. The coach then completes his technique checklist by evaluating the fielder's throwing mechanics.

*Coaching Points:*

- At the first checkpoint (the catch), the coach should check to make sure that the player is:
  - bending his knees.
  - keeping his back flat.
  - placing the heel of his throwing hand near the heel of his glove hand.
  - looking the ball into his glove.
- At the second checkpoint (the explosion), the coach should check to make sure that the player is:
  - replacing his left foot with his right foot (for the right-handed thrower).
  - bending his knees.
  - keeping his elbows at shoulder height.
  - posturing his shoulders so that an imaginary line runs straight through his shoulders to the target.

- At the third checkpoint (the throw), the coach should check to make sure that the player is:
  - moving his glove to the tuck position.
  - bringing his throwing hand forward on line to the target.
  - rotating his hips toward the target.
  - finishing the throw with his back parallel to the ground.
  - reaching for the ground as he follows through on the throw.
  - rolling his hips to finish the throw.

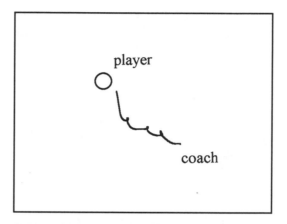

**Drill #29: Catch—Explode—Throw—Ground Ball Drill.**

## DRILL #30: 5-4-3 DOUBLE PLAY DRILL

*Objective:* To develop the third baseman's technique in turning a double play.

*Equipment Needed:* A crate of baseballs; a glove; a base.

*Location:* An infield.

*Description:* A feeder sits on a crate approximately 25 feet away from third base. The third baseman, a second baseman, and a first baseman assume the appropriate double-play positions. The feeder throws a regular ground ball to the third baseman. The third baseman should play the ball using the appropriate technique to field the specific type of ground ball that is being simulated by the feeder. (Refer to Drill #1— Triangle Drill—for coaching points on how to properly field the various types of ground balls.) Once the third baseman fields the ball, he should make a strong throw toward the chest of the second baseman. The second baseman should time his movement to second base so that his chest is over the base at the moment the ball is caught. This timing allows the second baseman to execute his proper footwork on a 5-4-3 double play. The footwork for the 5-4-3 double play involves the feet of a second baseman working in the following sequence: left foot in the middle of the bag, right foot in the dirt to the third-base side; left foot in the dirt to the first-base side. The second baseman should complete his footwork with a hop over an imaginary sliding baserunner. The second baseman can complete the play by either throwing to first, or making a simulated throw to first base if no player is covering first.

*Coaching Point:*

- The third baseman should stay low and whip his hips open when throwing to second base.

## DRILL #31: 3-6-3 DOUBLE PLAY DRILL

*Objective:* To refine the first-to-short and back-to-first double-play mechanics of the first baseman and the shortstop.

*Equipment Needed:* A crate of baseballs; a glove; two bases.

*Location:* An infield.

*Description:* A feeder kneels on the ground or sits on a crate near the first base-line, approximately 25 feet from the first baseman. The feeder throws a ground ball to the first baseman. Using the proper techniques, the first baseman should field the ground ball and throw the ball to the shortstop who is covering second base. The shortstop should move to cover second base, as the first baseman fields the ground ball. Once the first baseman releases the ball on his throw to second base, he should hustle to first base to position himself to receive the return throw from the shortstop.

*Coaching Points:*

- Both players should position themselves to the inside of the first-to-second baseline so that the runner advancing to second base doesn't interfere with the throw.
- If the first baseman is pulled too far off the bag to be able to cover first base, the pitcher should cover the bag, while the first baseman ducks to stay clear of the sight line between the shortstop and the pitcher.
- The throw should be made to the inside of the bags.

## DRILL #32: RUN DOWN DRILL

*Objective:* To practice the proper technique of a run down during a pick-off play.

*Equipment Needed:* One baseball; helmets for the baserunners; gloves for the infielders.

*Location:* The infield between two bases.

*Description:* A baserunner is positioned at first base. A feeder stationed on the infield, approximately 25 feet away from first base, throws the ball to the first baseman. As the feeder throws the ball, the baserunner breaks toward second base. The first baseman should catch the ball and make a quick throw to the shortstop. The shortstop should pinch (i.e., shorten the distance between second and first). If the shortstop is able to make the tag on the base runner, the drill is terminated. If the baserunner breaks back toward first base, the shortstop should sprint toward the baserunner while holding the ball in a throwing position above his shoulder. The shortstop should continue to chase the baserunner until the infielder covering first base yells "ball". When the covering infielder yells "ball", the chasing infielder should immediately throw the ball to the covering infielder.

*Coaching Points:*

- The infielders should throw the ball to the inside of the baseline.
- The chasing infielder should not fake throwing the ball in an attempt to get the baserunner to stop or hesitate.
- Run downs should be practiced with the middle infielders in various situations (e.g., between first and second base, between second and third base, and between third base and home plate).
- The shortstop should throw the ball to the first baseman if the baserunner turns his head away from him.
- The infielders' primary objective should be to complete the run down with as few throws as possible.

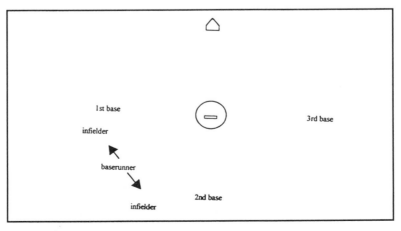

**Drill #32: Run Down Drill.**

## DRILL #33: TWO-LINE RUN DOWN DRILL

*Objective:* To practice the "ball" call and throw during the run-down drill.

*Equipment Needed:* One baseball; gloves for the infielders.

*Location:* Anywhere on the baseball field.

*Description:* The infielders form two lines. The head of each line stands approximately sixty feet apart. The coach selects one line to start the drill. The first person in that line then begins running toward the opposite line of players. The first player holds the ball in the ready position above his shoulder, while a player from the second line begins running toward him. As both players continue running toward each other and close to within a distance of 15 feet, the player without the ball should yell "ball." The first player should then throw the ball to the second player and peel off to return to the back of his line. The second player should catch the ball, while continuing forward. Another player from the first line should then replace the first player. When the two players close to a distance of 15 feet, the third player should call "ball," and the second player should throw the ball. The second player should then peel back to the end of his line, as a fourth player from his line replaces him. The drill should continue while the third player continues to close the distance between himself and the fourth player. The loop ends once every player has had the chance to act as a pitcher and a receiver of the throw.

*Coaching Points:*

- The players should not fake the throw.
- This drill is an excellent developmental drill to practice the run-down technique.

# CHAPTER 2

# DRILLS FOR CATCHERS

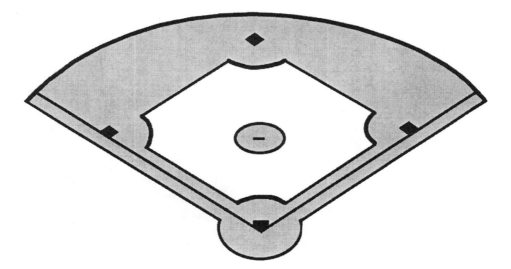

### DRILL #34: FRAMING WITH THE TENNIS BALL DRILL

*Objective:* To improve the catcher's framing ability.

*Equipment Needed:* A crate of tennis balls.

*Location:* Anywhere on the baseball field.

*Description:* The catcher squats in his catching stance. The coach kneels on the ground or sits on a crate approximately twenty feet away from the catcher. The coach throws the ball to each of the different areas of the strike zone. The catcher's glove hand is bare-handed. The catcher should catch the thrown ball and frame it. The catcher should hold his throwing hand behind his back. Framing is a technique used to bring a ball thrown outside of the strike zone into the strike zone, making the pitch appear to be a strike. When framing, the catcher should cushion the catch to his chest by allowing his hand and elbow to absorb the force of the ball. Framing involves the following techniques:

- If the ball is high, the catcher should snap his wrist downward and gently bring the ball toward his chest.
- If the ball is low, the catcher should move the ball upward and toward his chest.
- If the ball is inside, the catcher should rotate his catching hand in toward the strike zone, as he gently moves the ball toward his chest.
- If the ball is outside, the catcher should pop his wrist in toward the strike zone and gently bring the ball to his chest.

*Coaching Points:*

- The catcher should never frame a ball that is clearly outside the strike zone. Only pitches that are just outside of the strike zone should be framed.
- The catcher should cushion the pitch with his elbow and hand.
- The drill can be done with baseballs if the catcher uses a mitt.
- The drill can be performed with the catcher either in a normal catching stance if no runner is on base or in a stance appropriate for a situation in which a runner is on base.

**Drill #34: Framing with the Tennis Ball Drill.**

## DRILL #35: REPLACING THE FEET DRILL

*Objective:* To improve the catcher's footwork and ball delivery to a base.

*Equipment Needed:* A crate of baseballs.

*Location:* Home plate.

*Description:* The catcher squats in the appropriate stance for a situation that involves a baserunner. An appropriate stance for a right-handed catcher facing a baserunner is a stance in which his left foot is positioned slightly ahead of his right foot. His lower back should be arched so that his buttocks are prominent in the stance. His elbows should be flexed slightly, and his mitt should be held out from his body. He should hold his mitt chest-high with his right hand positioned in a fist behind his mitt. For safety, his right thumb should be tucked inside his fist. Once the catcher receives the pitch, he should rake the glove. Raking the glove entails moving the glove across his face toward his right ear. Raking the glove puts the catcher in the ideal throwing position. As the catcher rakes the glove, he should replace his feet. Replacing the feet is accomplished by snapping his left shoulder toward the target. His right foot then replaces his left foot as he moves to make the throw.

*Coaching Points:*

- When the catcher points his left shoulder to the target, an imaginary line can be drawn straight from his right elbow to his left elbow. The line should cut through his chest.
- Quickness in the foot-replacement stage of the catcher's set to throw is a key factor in his being able to make an effective delivery to a base. The quicker he replaces his feet, the quicker he can release the ball.

**Drill #35: Replacing the Feet Drill.** *Emphasis point: The catcher should replace his left foot with his right foot.*

## DRILL #36: BLOCKING DRILL

*Objective:* To improve the catcher's blocking technique.

*Equipment Needed:* A crate of baseballs; the catcher's protective gear.

*Location:* Home plate.

*Description:* The coach stands approximately twenty feet in front of home plate, as the catcher assumes the proper stance. The coach throws short hops to the catcher. When the ball hits in front of the catcher, he should drop to his knees and bring his glove to a position between his legs. He should keep his elbows tucked to his sides. The open side of the mitt should face the coach as the fingertips of both of his hands touch the ground. The catcher should use his chest to absorb the force of the ball, expelling air from his lungs as the ball hits his chest. If the ball bounces to one side of the catcher, the catcher should take a short lead step to the side of the ball and drop to his knees. When moving to one side, the catcher should turn his body inward so that the ball will ricochet toward the plate.

*Coaching Points:*

- The catcher should collapse his chest as the ball bounces toward him, then expel air from the lungs. This step causes the ball to lose kinetic energy and results in it dying near the catcher on the ricochet off his chest.
- This drill should be introduced in a slow and controlled manner.
- The speed of the ball thrown by the coach should be appropriate to the age and skill level of the catcher.

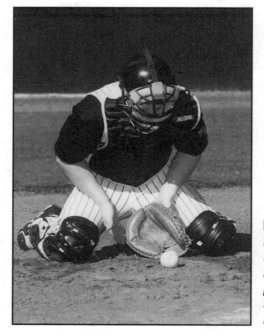

**Drill #36: Blocking Drill.**
***Emphasis point: The catcher should round his shoulders; his primary objective should be to block the ball—not to catch it.***

## DRILL #37: POINTING DRILL

*Objective:* To improve the catcher's quickness in his blocking technique.

*Equipment Needed:* A catcher's protective gear.

*Location:* Home plate.

*Description:* The catcher wears his full protective equipment and assumes the proper stance behind home plate. The coach stands in front of the catcher and directs the drill by pointing to one of three directions—to the right of the catcher, to the left of the catcher, and directly in front of the catcher. The catcher keeps his hands behind his back and responds to the coach's direction by moving to block an imaginary ball. When the coach points to one side of the catcher, the catcher should move and drop to block the imaginary short hop. The catcher should then immediately pop up and return to his catcher's stance behind home plate. The coach should then point to give the catcher another direction in which he should move to block the imaginary short hop. If the coach points to the ground in front of the catcher, the catcher should move forward and drop to block the imaginary short hop in front of him.

*Coaching Point:*

- The coach should control the tempo of the drill so that the catcher is moving quickly throughout the drill.

**Drill #37: Pointing Drill. *Emphasis point: The catcher should move in the direction that the coach points.***

## DRILL #38: BLOCKING THE CURVE BALL DRILL

*Objective:* To improve the catcher's blocking technique when facing a curve ball in the dirt.

*Equipment Needed:* A pitching machine; catcher's protective gear.

*Location:* Home plate.

*Description:* The coach sets the pitching machine to throw a curve ball. The pitching machine can simulate a curve ball from both a right-handed pitcher and a left-handed pitcher. When simulating a curve ball into the dirt from a left-handed pitcher, the rotation of the ball will cause the ball to bounce back to the catcher's right. When simulating a curve ball into the dirt from a right-handed pitcher, the rotation of the ball will cause the ball to bounce to the catcher's left side. Once the pitch is thrown, the catcher should attack the ball as soon as he realizes that is going to hit the dirt.

*Coaching Points:*

- For the full effect of a curve ball in the dirt, the pitching machine should be positioned on the mound.
- The catcher should be drilled to react to the dominant hand of a pitcher upon recognizing a ball into the dirt. The curve ball in the dirt will normally bounce toward the direction corresponding to the pitcher's throwing hand.

**Drill #38: Blocking the Curve Ball Drill.** *Emphasis point: The catcher should angle his body slightly toward the pitcher's throwing-hand side.*

## DRILL #39: POP-UP DRILL

*Objective:* To improve the catcher's technique when catching a pop up near home plate.

*Equipment Needed:* A pitching machine; a catcher's protective gear.

*Location:* Home plate.

*Description:* The pitching machine is placed near home plate as the catcher assumes his position behind the plate. The coach shoots the ball into the air. The catcher should immediately take off his mask and sprint in the direction where he suspects that the ball will fall. Once the catcher is convinced of the flight of the ball, he should throw his mask away in the opposite direction so that he won't trip over it. The catcher should always turn his back to the playing field to catch a pop fly. This position best allows the catcher to handle the spin of the ball when it is popped up . The catcher should catch the ball out in front of his body with his hands held above his head. Upon the ball contacting the glove, the catcher should cushion the ball's downward force with his hands and elbows. He should bend his knees to assume an athletic stance so that he can move with the wavering flight of the ball. A good athletic stance also helps the catcher wheel to throw the ball to a target point.

*Coaching Point:*

- The catcher should never allow the ball to drift behind his head. He should keep the ball in front of his body.

**Drill #39: Pop-Up Drill.**
*Emphasis point: The catcher should turn his back to the infield.*

**DRILL #40: THROW-DOWNS DRILL**

*Objective:* To improve the catcher's time in throwing to second base.

*Equipment Needed:* A crate of baseballs; a catcher's equipment; a stopwatch.

*Location:* The infield.

*Description:* Wearing his equipment, the catcher assumes his proper stance with an imaginary runner on first base. A feeder kneels midway between the mound and home plate. The feeder throws a pitch to the catcher. The catcher should attack the pitch using the proper techniques and make a low, hard throw to the inside of second base. The coach starts his stopwatch the moment the ball hits the catcher's glove and stops it the moment the middle infielder makes the catch. The coach should compute an average time for throwing to second base, using a cluster of throw-downs as a basis (i.e., five throw-downs, ten throw-downs, etc.).

*Coaching Points:*

- The ideal mitt-to-glove time for a top-level high school catcher is within the range of 2.0 to 2.2 seconds.
- The ideal mitt-to-glove time for a post-secondary level catcher is within the range of 1.8 to 2.0 seconds.
- The accuracy of the catcher's throw is equally important to the speed of the throw.
- The middle infielder should be able to make the catch as he straddles the base.
- The throw-down should be made to the middle infielder so that he can make a quick tag on the baserunner.

**Drill #40: Throw-downs Drill.**

## DRILL #41: FIELDING BUNTS DRILL

*Objective:* To improve the catcher's technique in fielding a bunt.

*Equipment Needed:* A crate of baseballs; a catcher's equipment.

*Location:* The infield.

*Description:* The catcher assumes the proper stance behind home plate. The coach stands behind the catcher and tosses a baseball in a random direction out from home plate. The catcher should explode out of his stance to the field the ball with his bare hand. If the ball is hit down the first base line, the catcher should field the ball and step to the inside of the base path to make a strong throw to first base. If the ball is bunted toward the pitching mound, the catcher should explode out of his stance and reverse out (i.e., half-spin) to field the ball and throw to first base. In reversing out, the catcher should keep his feet shoulder width apart and field the ball off his back foot. A right-handed catcher should get his left shoulder around to point at first base prior to releasing the ball. The catcher should use the reverse-out fielding technique anytime the ball is bunted to the third-base side of the mound.

*Coaching Points:*

- When reversing-out, the catcher should turn his back to the fielders as he secures the ball.
- When fielding the ball, the catcher should use his "whole hand" and push down on the ball as he grasps it.

**Drill #41: Fielding Bunts Drill.** *Emphasis point: The catcher should reverse out on a ball to the left of the pitching mound.*

## DRILL #42: BACKING-UP FIRST BASE DRILL

*Objective:* To improve the catcher's technique in backing-up first base.

*Equipment Needed:* Catcher's equipment.

*Location:* Home plate and first-base foul territory.

*Description:* Wearing his equipment, the catcher assumes his proper stance behind home plate. On the coach's command, the catcher should sprint to a location between first base and the dugout. The catcher should get as close to first base as he can without jeopardizing his ability to stop a wild throw to first base. He cannot allow a wild throw to first base to fly over his head or roll by him.

*Coaching Point:*

- The catcher should remove his mask and toss it out of his way as he sprints to first base.

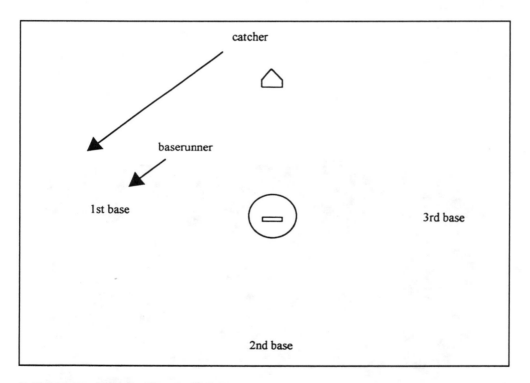

**Drill #42: Backing-Up First Base Drill.**

## DRILL #43: WILD PITCH DRILL

*Objective:* To improve the catcher's technique in responding to a wild pitch that goes to the backstop.

*Equipment Needed:* Catcher's equipment; a crate of baseballs.

*Location:* Home plate.

*Description:* Wearing his equipment, the catcher assumes his proper stance behind home plate. The coach stands on the grass in front of home plate and throws a ball past the catcher toward the backstop. The catcher should turn to the side of the wild pitch and sprint to the ball. To field the ball, the catcher should round the point at where the ball will stop. As the catcher closes to the ball, he should slide to the ground on his left knee and extend his right leg. He should use his "whole hand" to grasp the ball from the turf and pop up from his left knee to a throwing position. A proper throwing position for the right-handed catcher is a position in which his left shoulder is pointed at the target.

*Coaching Points:*

- The coach should throw the ball in various directions toward the backstop.
- The catcher should not turn to field the ball until the ball is past him.
- The ideal throwing position for a catcher in this situation is a position in which an imaginary line runs from the catcher's throwing elbow to the target. The line should travel through the catcher's chest and the elbow of his glove-hand arm.

**Drill #43: Wild Pitch Drill. *Emphasis point: The catcher should slide on one knee with his other leg extended, reaching for the ball with an open hand.***

## DRILL #44: PICKOFFS TO FIRST BASE DRILL

*Objective:* To improve the catcher's technique in throwing to first base on a pickoff.

*Equipment Needed:* Catcher's equipment; a crate of baseballs.

*Location:* Home plate and first base.

*Description:* Wearing his equipment, the catcher assumes his proper stance behind home plate for a situation in which a runner is on first base. A coach stands midway between the pitching mound and home plate and throws balls to the catcher. A right-handed catcher should pivot on his right foot and step with his left foot to first base. The catcher should use the raking technique to bring the ball to a throwing position and make a strong throw to first base.

*Coaching Points:*

- Against a left-handed batter, the catcher should step behind the batter to deliver the ball to first base.
- A right-handed catcher should drive his left shoulder toward the ground when throwing the ball to first base.

## DRILL #45: PICKOFFS TO THIRD BASE DRILL

*Objective:* To improve the catcher's technique in throwing to third base on a pickoff.

*Equipment Needed:* Catcher's equipment; a crate of baseballs.

*Location:* Home plate and third base.

*Description:* Wearing his equipment, the catcher assumes his proper stance behind home plate for a situation in which a runner is on third base. A coach stands midway between the pitching mound and home plate and throws balls to the catcher. A right-handed catcher should use the "replace-feet" technique as he throws to third base. The catcher should use the raking technique to bring the ball to a throwing position and make a strong throw to third base.

*Coaching Points:*

- Against a right-handed batter, the catcher should step behind the batter to deliver the ball to third base.
- A right-handed catcher should throw to the inside of the third base bag.
- A right-handed catcher should drive his left shoulder toward the ground when throwing the ball to first base.

**Drill #45: Pickoffs to Third Base Drill.**

# CHAPTER 3

# DRILLS FOR OUTFIELDERS

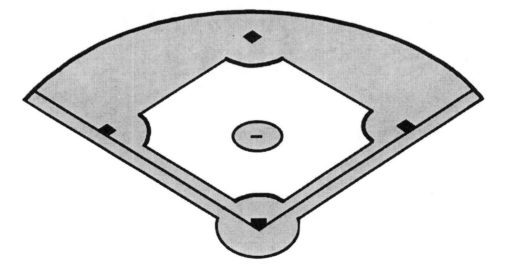

## DRILL #46: FACE DRILL

*Objective:* To improve the outfielder's technique of opening his body to catch a fly ball hit to each of the three basic fielding spots—to his right; to his left; and over his head.

*Equipment Needed:* A crate of baseballs.

*Location:* Outfield.

*Description:* The coach stands approximately twenty feet away as the outfielder assumes a ready position. A proper ready position for a right-handed outfielder is a position in which the outfielder staggers his left foot slightly ahead of his right foot. The coach throws the ball to one of the three spots. The coach should either throw the ball as a line drive or a fly ball. When fielding a fly ball, an outfielder's first step should be in the direction in which the ball is heading. When fielding a line drive, the outfielder should use a cross-over technique as his initial step.

*Coaching Points:*

- To ensure that the outfielder is not taking false steps, the coach should fake throws to different directions.
- The outfielder should explode out of the ready position to field the ball.

## DRILL #47: BALL—TAKE IT DRILL

*Objective:* To teach the proper communication in the situation of a fly ball hit between two outfielders.

*Equipment Needed:* A crate of baseballs; a fungo bat.

*Location:* Outfield.

*Description:* The three outfielders align in their normal positions in the outfield. The centerfielder takes the middle position, while the left fielder and right fielder align in their respective positions. The coach hits a fly ball between two of the fielders. Both players then break to field the ball. The outfielder who feels confident that he can field the ball should yell "ball—ball." The second outfielder should yield to the outfielder making the call. As the second outfielder yields, he should yell "take it—take it" to the first outfielder. The first outfielder to yell "ball—ball" should be given the right of way. Should both outfielders simultaneously make the call for the ball, the centerfielder should be awarded the right of way.

*Coaching Points:*

- The second outfielder should move to back-up the outfielder calling "ball—ball."
- If an outfielder and an infielder simultaneously call for a fly ball during a game, the infielder should yield the right-of-way to the outfielder.
- If an outfielder realizes that he can't make the catch after he has yelled "ball—ball," he should immediately yell "take it—take it" to his teammate and yield the right-of-way.

## DRILL #48: CROW HOP GROUND BALL DRILL

*Objective:* To develop the outfielder's crow hop technique when fielding a ground ball

*Equipment Needed:* A crate of baseballs; a fungo bat.

*Location:* Outfield.

*Description:* Standing on the right field foul line, the coach hits a ground ball to an outfielder who is positioned in centerfield. The outfielder should sprint to the hit ball and breakdown to field it. When fielding a ground ball, the outfielder should catch the ball in front of the foot corresponding to his glove-hand. After securing the ball in his glove, the outfielder should crow hop to utilize his forward momentum to make his throw. To crow hop, the right-handed outfielder should step with his right foot to square his body to the directional point where he wants to throw the ball. After squaring his body, the right-handed outfielder should step forward with his left foot. The right-left combination steps create a crow-hopping motion as the outfielder continues forward. The outfielder can finish the drill by faking the throw.

*Coaching Points:*

- The proper fielding technique for a ground ball involves bending the knees, keeping the back parallel to the ground, and watching the ball roll into the glove.
- Upon securing the ball, the outfielder should explode forward. An inexperienced outfielder tends to improperly pop upward.
- A key element to the crow-hop technique is the outfielder's quickness in squaring off with the foot corresponding to his throwing hand and stepping into the hop with his glove-side foot.
- Having the outfielder fake the throw eliminates the need for a cutoff man, reduces the incidence of sore arms, and gives the outfielders more repetitions.

**Drill #48: Crow Hop Ground Ball Drill.**
*Emphasis point: The outfielder should square off his back foot to the target.*

## DRILL #49: CROW HOP FLY BALL DRILL

*Objective:* To develop the outfielder's crow hop technique when fielding a fly ball.

*Equipment Needed:* A crate of baseballs; a fungo bat.

*Location:* Outfield.

*Description:* Standing on the right-field foul line, the coach hits a fly ball to an outfielder who is positioned in centerfield. The coach alternates hitting pop-ups and line drives. The outfielder should field the ball and finish the drill with a crow-hop technique. He may fake a throw or make a throw to a cutoff man. When fielding a fly ball with a runner on base, the outfielder should round the ball and square off with their back foot before as they initiate the crow hop. (Refer to Drill #48 for more details additional guidelines on how to properly crow hop).

*Coaching Points:*

- The crow hop drill can be done inside a gymnasium, with the outfielder simulating the catching of a ball and throwing the ball against the wall.
- The coach should make sure that an outfielder squares his stance as he initiates his crow hop.

**Drill #48: Crow Hop Fly Ball Drill. *Emphasis point: The outfielder should square off his back foot to the target, and point his front shoulder to the target.***

## DRILL #50: TEAM POP-UP DRILL

*Objective:* To simulate game conditions for players fielding a pop-up fly ball.

*Equipment Needed:* A crate of baseballs; a fungo bat.

*Location:* The entire field.

*Description:* All nine players take their positions in the field. Standing at home plate, the coach hits randomly placed pop-ups. The player who is in the best position for catching the ball should yell "ball—ball—ball." The other players nearby should respond to the player's call by yelling" take it—take it. The player to whom the ball is hit should catch it and throw it back to the coach.

*Coaching Points:*

- Outfielders have the right-of-way when the ball is hit in the hole between the infield and outfield.
- Infielders have the right-of-way over the pitcher and the catcher when a fly ball is hit in the infield.

## DRILL #51: DIVE DRILL

*Objective:* To develop the outfielder's technique in diving for a fly ball.

*Equipment Needed:* A crate of baseballs; a fungo bat.

*Location:* Outfield.

*Description:* The coach stands approximately twenty feet away, as the outfielder assumes a ready position. A proper ready position for a right-handed outfielder is a position in which the player staggers his left foot slightly ahead of his right foot. The coach should progressively build the players' diving technique by throwing the ball just out of the outfielder's reach. After the players master the technique of diving for a thrown ball, the coach hits fungo fly balls. When sprinting to a fly ball, the outfielder should not hold his glove out. He should wait for the last moment to reach out and snag the ball with his glove. The coach may hit fungo from either the right field line or left field line. The outfielder can be positioned in centerfield when the coach hits fungo from the foul line.

*Coaching Point:*

- The proper technique for diving involves having the player land on his stomach.

**Drill #51: Dive Drill. *Emphasis point: When diving for a fly ball, the outfielder should make his body parallel with the ground.***

## DRILL #52: TRASH CAN THROWING DRILL

*Objective:* To develop the outfielder's accuracy when throwing a ball to home plate.

*Equipment Needed:* A crate of baseballs; a fungo bat; three 50-gallon trash cans or barrels.

*Location:* Outfield.

*Description:* Three trash cans are positioned in the infield as the players take their positions in the outfield. The trash cans are positioned in an arc—one in front of home plate between home plate and the mound, one between the mound and the first base line, and one between the mound and third base line. The coach stands near home plate and hits either a ground ball or a fly ball to the outfield. The outfielders should then demonstrate the proper mechanics for catching the ball and crow hopping. The outfielder should make a strong throw to home plate. The coach should emphasis throwing accuracy to the players and count how many times a player hits the trash can during a specific number of throws.

*Coaching Point:*

- Emphasis should be placed on every player adhering to the proper fundamentals when fielding either a ground ball or a fly ball.

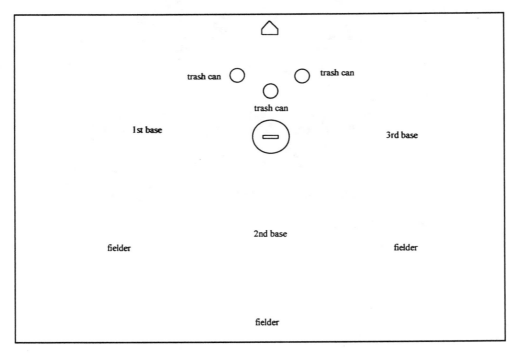

**Drill #52: Trash Can Throwing Drill.**

## DRILL #53: WALL DRILL

*Objective:* To develop the outfielder's ability to catch a fly ball against the outfield wall.

*Equipment Needed:* A crate of baseballs.

*Location:* Outfield wall.

*Description:* A player stands on the front edge of the warning track, approximately 15 feet from the outfield wall. The player faces home plate as he stands in the ready position. Standing in front of the player, the coach throws a fly ball to the upper edge of the wall. The outfielder should react by opening his hips to the side where the ball is hit and sprinting to the wall. When entering the warning track, the outfielder should glance at the wall to check his distance, then resight the flight of the ball. As the ball nears the outfielder, he should reach for the wall with his hand. The outfielder should then jump vertically, not horizontally, to catch the fly ball going over the wall.

*Coaching Point:*

- The players should walk through this drill until they are proficient at reaching for the wall and resighting a fly ball.

**Drill #53: Wall Drill.**

## DRILL #54: CUTOFF DRILL

*Objective:* To develop the outfielder's accuracy when throwing a ball to a cutoff man.

*Equipment Needed:* A crate of baseballs; a fungo bat.

*Location:* The entire baseball field.

*Description:* Each of the nine players takes his position in the field. Standing near home plate, the coach hits fly balls and ground balls to the outfield. On a ball hit to the outfield, the appropriate infielder should sprint toward the outfield and function as a cutoff man. The cutoff man positions himself so that the outfielder can make a strong throw on a straight line to him. How deep a cutoff man sets up in the outfield depends on two factors—the distance of the fly ball and the strength of the outfielder's arm. The further the ball is hit, the deeper in the outfield the cutoff man should set up. If the outfielder's has a strong arm, the cutoff man may need to only move slightly into the outfield grass. Once the cutoff man sets up at the proper depth, he should raise his hands to alert the outfielder. The outfielder should throw to the cutoff man who has both hands raised.

*Coaching Points:*

- The cutoff technique is designed so the player with the stronger arm makes the longer throw in the relay.
- Verbal commands, along with hand signals, should be used in directing the outfielder's throw.

## JUDGEMENT AND THROWING

### DRILL #55: PASSING ROUTE DRILL

*Objective:* To develop the outfielder's ability to judge the flight of a fly ball and move to make the catch.

*Equipment Needed:* A crate of baseballs.

*Location:* Outfield.

*Description:* Both the coach and the outfielder face the same direction. On the coach's command, the outfielder should sprint deep into the outfield. At that point, the coach throws the ball to the outfielder. The distance the outfielder runs depends on the flight of the ball. The coach's throw should lead the player so that he has to continue running in order to make the catch. The outfielder should look back over his shoulder for the ball as he runs. Once the coach releases the ball, the outfielder should judge where the ball will land (he should take his eyes off the ball to look at that spot). He should then adjust his angle of pursuit to get to that spot. Once he nears the spot, he should look up for the ball as he sets up to make the catch.

*Coaching Points:*

- The player should be thrown fly balls to his left, to his right, and over his head.
- This drill is an excellent vehicle for addressing the conditioning factor in the outfielders.

## DRILL #56: DO OR DIE FLY BALL DRILL

*Objective:* To simulate catching a fly ball with a game-tying or a go-ahead base runner on third base.

*Equipment Needed:* A crate of baseballs; a fungo bat; a batting helmet for the base runner.

*Location:* The entire baseball field.

*Description:* Each of the nine players takes his position in the field. A runner is positioned on third base. Standing near home plate, the coach hits shallow fly balls into the outfield. The outfielder should posture himself so that he catches the ball as he is moving forward—toward home plate. The baserunner should tag up and sprint for home plate as the outfielder makes the catch. The outfielder should make the throw to home plate so that the catcher can make the tag on the base runner.

*Coaching Points:*

- The outfielder should "round the ball"—positioning his body so that the ball is caught on the side of his throwing arm.
- The outfielder should throw through the cutoff man. The cutoff man for the right fielder and the center fielder is the first baseman. The cutoff man for the left fielder is the third baseman.
- It is important that the outfielder is moving forward when catching the ball.
- Several players should be utilized as baserunners in this drill so that the baserunner is always relatively fresh.

## DRILL #57: DO OR DIE GROUND BALL DRILL

*Objective:* To simulate catching a ground ball with a game-tying or go-ahead base runner on second base.

*Equipment Needed:* A crate of baseballs; a fungo bat; a batting helmet for the baserunner.

*Location:* Baseball field.

*Description:* Each of the nine players takes his position in the field. A runner is positioned on second base. The coach hits a ground ball to a particular outfielder. The baserunner takes off for home when he sees the ground ball hit. The outfielder to whom the ball is hit should attack the grounder and position himself so that he fields the ball using the proper technique. The proper technique entails that the outfielder scoop the ball from a spot slightly forward and to the outside of his glove hand. After quickly retrieving the ball from his glove, the outfielder should throw the ball to home plate, aiming his throw at a point through the cutoff man.

*Coaching Points:*

- The outfielder should throw through the cutoff man. The cutoff man for the right fielder and the center fielder is the first baseman. The cutoff man for the left fielder is the third baseman.
- Several players should be utilized as baserunners for this drill so that the baserunner is always relatively fresh.

**DRILL #58: POSITIONING DRILL**

*Objective:* To improve outfielder's technique in positioning his body to make a strong throw.

*Equipment Needed:* A crate of baseballs; a fungo bat; three empty crates.

*Location:* Baseball field.

*Description:* The outfielders go to their respective positions. A coach stands near home plate and hits a fly ball to an outfielder. The outfielder should round the ball to make the catch. As he makes the catch, the outfielder should continue two steps toward the target. The player should catch the ball out in front of his body and above his head. He should not stop moving as he catches the ball, but run through the catch. The outfielder should finish with a crow hop and a fake throw.

*Coaching Points:*

- If the outfielder catches the ball on the side of his throwing arm, he should use two hands to catch the ball.

- The outfielder should practice catching a fly ball thrown to either side of his body, as well as directly to him.

- The outfielder should place the ball in the crate after faking the throw.

## DRILL #59: LONG TOSS DRILL

*Objective:* To improve outfielder's arm strength and throwing accuracy.

*Equipment Needed:* One baseball per group.

*Location:* Outfield.

*Description:* Two players stand approximately one hundred feet apart and toss the ball back and forth between them. The player throwing the ball should throw the ball so that the receiving player doesn't have to take more than one step to catch it The player making the throw should retreat two steps after making the throw. The player should throw the ball with a flat trajectory—never higher than twenty feet. When throwing the ball, the player should execute the crow hop toward his teammate.

*Coaching Points:*

- This drill can be structured as a competitive game. Whenever a player receiving the throw has to step more than one step, the player who threw the ball is cut from the game. In this scenario, the drill should then end when one player is left.
- The player should use a four-seam grip on the ball.
- When throwing the ball with a four-seam grip, the player should keep his fingers on top of the ball.

# CHAPTER 4

# HITTING DRILLS

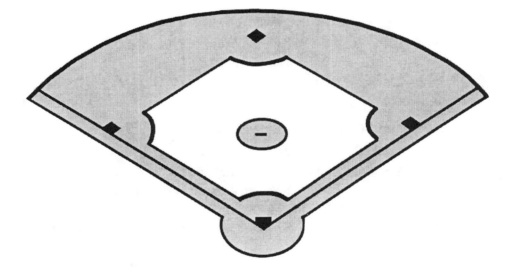

### DRILL #60: ONE -TWO -THREE DRILL

*Objective:* To teach the five sequential components to hitting: stance; rhythm; load; fire; and follow through.

*Equipment Needed:* A bat.

*Location:* Anywhere.

*Description:* The first of the five sequential components demonstrated by the effective hitter is the stance. The player should assume a comfortable batting stance. A good batting stance exhibits the following characteristics:

- Feet should be slightly wider than shoulder-width—wide enough to form a solid base.
- Knees should be flexed
- Shoulders should be level.
- Hands should be in front of his back shoulder.
- Rearward shoulder should be positioned behind the back foot.
- Wrists should be cocked and his hands should be relaxed.
- Rearward elbow should be down.
- Hips should be level.
- Feet should be pointing toward the plate.
- Eyes should be level and focused on the pitcher.

The second of the five sequential components is the hitter's rhythm. A hitter's rhythm is an established set of movements (i.e., a ritual) that the batter performs prior to loading his stance. An example of a movement in this situation is the hitter wiggling his bat over the plate to distract the sign communication between the catcher and the pitcher.

The third of the five sequential components is the hitter's load. When loading, the batter shifts his weight backward. His hands move back in his stance, but his shoulders remain taut and straight. His wrists cock the bat. This action enables the batter to form the letter "C" with his hands and wrists as the barrel of the bat tilts slightly toward the pitcher. The batter should keep his hips level. His chin should be level, as his eyes focus on the pitcher.

The fourth of the five sequential components is the hitter's fire. In the fire stage, the batter's lower body should "trigger" (i.e., firing the back knee inward toward the ball) his forward movement. His front leg should flex, then replace his front foot (i.e., the hitter flexes his knee and lifts his foot slightly off the ground, then quickly returns his foot to the ground). His hips should rotate as his weight shifts forward. On the approach to the ball, the hitter should keep the bathead above his hands. His eyes should track the ball to the bat. His back elbow should enter the slot (i.e., the area near the side of the body).

The fifth of the five sequential components is the hitter's follow through. On the batter's follow through, the batter's hands should move forward toward the ball without fading away from his body. When the bat contacts the ball, the hitter's hands should be in a palm-up and palm-down relationship. His front elbow should pull down as his back elbow slides forward in the slot. Having the batter slide his back elbow forward in the slot brings his elbow towards his belly button. His arm should be parallel to the ground. The hitter should finish his swing with his chest facing the pitcher on an inside pitch and facing first base on an outside pitch. On the other hand, he should rotate his chest when executing the hitting motion (i.e., over-rotate). His back foot should finish on the two cleats that are located on the ball of his foot. The bat should finish with a follow-through after contact—swinging through to the opposite shoulder.

The drill begins by having the hitter assume the proper stance and perform his rhythm. The coach calls out, "one"—the hitter should execute a load technique. When the coach calls "two"—the hitter should begin his fire technique. Finally, when the coach calls "three"—the hitter should finish with his follow-through.

*Coaching Points:*

- The batter should keep his knees inside his feet.
- The batter should stand tall. He should not lean in his stance.
- The batter should not over-rotate. He should stay parallel to the path of the ball.
- The hitter's back knee and hip should explode through the ball.
- The batter's front knee should be flexed, yet should serve as a brace to facilitate a solid hit through the ball.

**DRILL #61: HITTING ZONE DRILL**

*Objective:* To develop the hitting technique against a pitch into each of the three different hitting zones—inside; outside; and down the middle.

*Equipment Needed:* A crate of baseballs.

*Location:* Home plate.

*Description:* The hitter assumes a batting stance while holding a ball in his top hand. Keeping in mind the five sequential components of an effective hitter's swing, the batter throws a ball instead of swinging a bat. His back arm and elbow should move into the slot, with his front arm moving parallel to the ground. The hitter should visualize slamming a door with his back arm and hand. The player should release the ball once his elbow moves into the slot. The batter's lower body should rotate before his arm moves into the slot. To simulate hitting a pitch down the middle, the player should throw to the pitcher's mound. To simulate hitting an inside pitch, the player should aim his throw at the closest base. For example, a right-handed hitter should aim for third base. To simulate an outside pitch, the player should throw the ball toward the base furthest from him. For example, in this instance, a right-handed hitter should aim for first base.

*Coaching Points:*

- On the outside pitch, the player's hips should not rotate. On both the inside pitch and a pitch down the middle, the player's chest should face the pitcher.

- How far the ball should be thrown depends on the strength and technique of the hitter. A high school player should be able to reach the infield dirt.

- To advance the drill to a higher level, the hitter can be required to throw to the shortstop and second base areas on command.

- The slot is the area located on to the right of a right-hander hitter—near his hip, ribs, and stomach.

**Drill #61: Hitting Zone Drill. *Emphasis point: The hitter's back elbow should move into slot position, parallel with the ground.***

## DRILL #62: BOUNCING BALL DRILL

*Objective:* To develop the hitter's ability to wait for a pitch and increase his effectiveness against an off-speed pitch.

*Equipment Needed:* A crate of tennis balls; a bat.

*Location:* Batting cage.

*Description:* The player assumes a hitting stance. A feeder sits in a chair behind a screen and throws a tennis ball toward the hitter. Upon its arrival in his hitting zone, the batter should hit the ball. The ball should be thrown so that it bounces before it gets to the hitter. The speed of the bounces should vary. The feeder should change the angle of his arm so that the hitter can't tell what type of pitch is coming.

*Coaching Points:*

- This drill develops the hitter's ability to be patient and keep the weight on his back leg.
- To increase the difficulty of the drill, the feeder should occasionally throw a ball to the hitter without bouncing it on the ground.
- The distance between the hitter and the feeder should vary according to the age and skill level of the participants.

**Drill #62: Bouncing Ball Drill.** *Emphasis point: The fielder should bounce a tennis ball to the hitter from behind a protective screen.*

**DRILL #63: HITTING DROP DRILL**

*Objective:* To improve the hitter's hand quickness.

*Equipment Needed:* Whiffle golf balls; a bat or a wooden stick; a temporary home plate.

*Location:* Anywhere on the field.

*Description:* Using a regulation bat or a stick cut to the length of a bat, the player assumes a hitting stance. The feeder stands a safe distance from the hitter, but close enough to be able to drop a whiffle golf ball into one of the three hitting zones. The feeder should be able to drop a ball that simulates either an inside pitch, an outside pitch, or a pitch down the middle. To drop the whiffle golf ball into the batter's inside hitting zone, the feeder should drop the ball in front of the hitter at a point on the inside corner of the plate. To drop the whiffle golf ball into the outside hitting zone, the feeder should drop the ball in front of the hitter to the batter's outside corner of the plate. To drop the whiffle golf ball into the middle of the batter's hitting zone, the feeder should drop the ball in front of the hitter at a point in the middle of the plate.

*Coaching Points:*

- The feeder should hold the ball in clear view of the hitter, using two or three fingers.
- The feeder should not toss the ball. He should simply drop the ball.
- To improve the difficulty level of the drill, the hitter should use a wooden stick or broom handle instead of a bat.

**Drill #63: Hitting Drop Drill.**

## DRILL #64: FENCE DRILL

*Objective:* To improve the hitter's technique so that his front arm doesn't extend outward during his swing.

*Equipment Needed:* A bat.

*Location:* Along a fence or a wall.

*Description:* A player stands facing the fence. To measure the appropriate distance from the fence, he touches the barrel of his bat to the fence and holds it parallel to the ground with the knob of the bat touching his navel. The player should remain at this distance from the fence and assume a hitting stance. He should move through the five components of an effective hitting technique. If the player's bat hits the fence, he is extending his front arm (which is a technique flaw). The player should continue the drill until he develops the proper technique of keeping his front elbow bent and his hands close to his body as he swings at an imaginary ball.

*Coaching Points:*

- The player should start the drill slowly so that he doesn't damage his bat.
- As the player feels comfortable in mastering the proper technique of the swing, he should increase the speed of his bat.
- The batter's back elbow should be kept in the slot as his lead elbow is flexed.
- The hitter should not step backward or outward as he swings the bat.

**Drill #64: Fence Drill.**

## DRILL #65: FENCE DRILL WITH WHIFFLE BALLS

*Objective:* To train the hitter to not extend outward during his swing.

*Equipment Needed:* A wooden broom stick cut the length of his bat; a crate of whiffle balls.

*Location:* A fence or wall.

*Description:* This drill is set up in the same way as Drill #64 (Fence Drill). This drill, however, involves a feeder who sits or kneels on a crate 15-20 feet in front of the hitter. The feeder throws whiffle balls to the hitter as the hitter swings the stick. The hitter should swing the stick just as he would swing a bat in a game situation. If he extends his arms outward on his swing, the hitter will strike the wall with the stick (which is a technique flaw).

*Coaching Points:*

- The hitter should take a normal swing at the ball.
- The batter's back elbow should be kept in the slot as his lead elbow is flexed.
- The hitter should not step out as he swings.
- As a rule, the feeder should not vary the speed of the ball.

**DRILL #66: SINGLE TEE DRILL**

*Objective:* To improve the hitter's swing and sense of contact with the ball in the three hitting zones.

*Equipment Needed:* A single batting tee; a plate; a crate of baseballs; a bat.

*Location:* A batting cage or a soft-toss hitting area.

*Description:* Standing in the batter's box so that he straddles the plate, the hitter should assume a proper batting stance and "measure up." To measure up, the batter reaches out with his bat and touches the opposite side of the plate. The batter then hits the ball off of a batting tee that is positioned according to what hitting zone he is attempting to work on. The tee is positioned for an inside pitch by placing it in front of the plate and on the inside corner. The tee is positioned for an outside pitch by placing it outside the plate, just off the back corner of the plate. To simulate a pitch down the middle, the tee is positioned directly in front of the plate.

*Coaching Points:*

- The hitter should demonstrate the five sequential components of the effective swing.
- Since most pitchers—particularly at the high school level—attempt to work hitters "away," the batter should have significantly more repetitions at hitting a simulated outside pitch.

**Drill #66: Single Tee Drill.**

## DRILL #67: STRAIGHT TO THE BALL DRILL

*Objective:* To eliminate the loop in the hitter's swing.

*Equipment Needed:* Two single batting tees; a crate of baseballs.

*Location:* A batting cage or a soft toss hitting area.

*Description:* Two tees are positioned one in front of the other. The back tee is positioned either higher or lower than the front tee. Strictly adhering to the five sequential components of an effective swing, the hitter swings at a baseball that has been placed on the front tee. The hitter's bat should not strike the back tee.

*Coaching Points:*

- The tees should be positioned so that the hitter practices hitting a ball in each of the three hitting zones.
- The hitter should keep the head of his bat up as long as possible.
- The drill may be done with a double tee instead of two single tees.
- If the player hits the ball on the back tee as he swings, he is dropping the barrel of the bat.

**Drill #67: Straight to the Ball Drill.** *Emphasis point: The hitter should quickly downward arch his bat to clear the back tee.*

## DRILL #68: DOUBLE TEE DRILL

*Objective:* To develop the hitter's technique in coverage on the corners of the plate.

*Equipment Needed:* Two single batting tees; a plate; a crate of baseballs.

*Location:* A batting cage or a soft toss hitting area.

*Description:* One tee is positioned on the front outside corner of the plate while the second tee is placed on the inside corner approximately six to eight inches in front of the first tee. A ball is put on each tee. The batter assumes his stance and loads. The coach, or hitting partner, calls out "inside" or "outside" when the batter loads to swing. The batter should then hit the ball off the tee that corresponds to the coach's command.

*Coaching Points:*

- Because many pitchers throw away (i.e., to the outside), most of the repetitions should involve hitting the ball off the outside tee.
- A ball should be placed on each tee for each repetition.

**Drill #68: Double Tee Drill.**

### DRILL #69: KNEE DRILL

*Objective:* To develop the upper body technique of the hitter.

*Equipment Needed:* A T-ball bat; a crate of baseballs.

*Location:* A batting cage or a soft toss screen.

*Description:* The hitter kneels on his back knee. He holds the bat in one hand, while he places his other hand across his chest. A feeder kneels near the hitter and tosses the ball to specific points. To simulate an inside pitch, the feeder tosses the ball to the hitter's inside knee. To simulate an outside pitch, the feeder tosses the ball to the hitter's back leg. To simulate a pitch down the middle, the feeder tosses the ball to the hitter's belt buckle. The hitter should hit the ball with only one hand on the bat. This drill is designed to isolate the upper body technique of the effective swing. It is also designed to improve the hitter's level of bat control.

*Coaching Points:*

- The hitter should keep his balance when swinging the bat.
- The hitter's head, eyes, and shoulders should remain level.
- The hitter should use his top hand to hold the bat when working on the inside pitch and his bottom hand when working on an outside pitch.

**Drill #69: Knee Drill.**

## DRILL #70: SOFT TOSS STICK DRILL

*Objective:* To develop the hitter's hand-eye coordination.

*Equipment Needed:* A crate of whiffle golf balls; a wooden broom handle cut to the length of a bat.

*Location:* Anywhere on the field.

*Description:* The batter assumes his hitting stance. A feeder should kneel on one knee approximately eight feet away from the batter. The feeder kneels in front of the batter, positioning himself at a slight angle from the hitter, while holding the ball firmly with all five of his fingers. The feeder should deliver the ball to the hitter by pulling his arm back and under-hand tossing the ball to the hitter. To simulate an inside pitch, the feeder tosses the ball to the hitter's front knee. To simulate an outside pitch, the feeder tosses the ball to the hitter's back knee. To simulate the pitch down the middle, the feeder tosses the ball toward the hitter's belt buckle. The primary objective of the hitter should be to hit line drives into the net.

*Coaching Points:*

- The drill may be done with a regulation bat and baseballs, provided the feeder is adequately protected from being injured.
- The hitter should keep his weight on his back leg.
- The hitter should keep his hands back.

## DRILL #71: MINI HEAT DRILL

*Objective:* To develop the hitter's bat speed.

*Equipment Needed:* A protective screen; a crate of whiffle golf balls; a wooden broom handle cut to the length of a bat.

*Location:* A batting cage.

*Description:* A feeder sits on a chair behind a protective screen. The hitter assumes a batting stance approximately fifteen feet away. The feeder throws pitches to each of the batter's three hitting zones. The batter should attempt to hit the thrown ball. The hitter should quickly cock his wrists in order to make solid contact with the ball. The drill can be done with the hitter using a regulation bat against either a whiffle golf ball or a baseball.

*Coaching Points:*

- Because the feeder is fairly close to the hitter, the hitter is literally forced to develop a "faster bat."
- The hitter should keep his hands close to his body.
- The hitter's elbows should be flexed until the bat contacts the ball.
- The batter's back elbow should move through the slot.

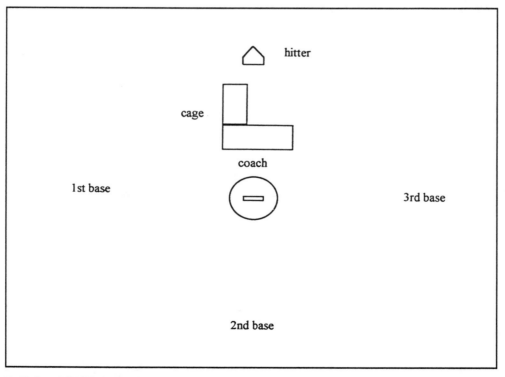

**Drill #71: Mini Heat Drill.**

## DRILL #72: CHECK ON CONTACT DRILL

*Objective:* To develop the hitter's technique when contacting the ball.

*Equipment Needed:* A protective screen; a crate of baseballs; a bat.

*Location:* A batting cage.

*Description:* The batter assumes a good hitting stance. From behind a protective screen, the feeder throws a pitch to one of the batter's three hitting zones. The hitter should swing his bat at the pitch, but stop the motion of the bat just at the moment of contact with the ball. The coach should then evaluate the check points of the batter's swing. The check points for a proper swing include the following:

- Keeping the back elbow in the slot.
- Keeping the palm-up and palm-down hand positioning.
- Keeping the head, eyes, and shoulders level.
- Keeping the hips level.
- Keeping the back foot pointed inward.
- Keeping the back knee slightly rotated inward.

*Coaching Point:*

- The coach should instruct the player on how to self-check his own swing.

## DRILL #73: WEIGHT SHIFT BOARD DRILL

*Objective:* To develop the hitter's technique of shifting his weight.

*Equipment Needed:* A balance board; a crate of baseballs; a bat.

*Location:* A batting cage.

*Description:* The batter assumes a proper hitting stance on the weight-shift board. The board should be tilted with the player placing most of his weight on his back leg. The hitter should stride into a pitch to hit the ball. The board should not move as the batter strides on his front leg. As the hitter enters the follow-through stage of his swing, he should shift his weight forward. The front portion of the board should slam down to the ground as the hitter follows through. The pitches are made by a feeder who is positioned behind a screen located approximately twenty feet away from the hitter.

*Coaching Points:*

- The hitter should be allowed an opportunity to familiarize himself with shifting his weight on the board.

- The front part of the board should not slam downward before the swing. If it does, this is an indication that the batter has improperly shifted his weight.

**Drill #73: Weight Shift Board Drill.** *Emphasis point: The hitter should assume the load position.*

**DRILL #74: BUNTING DRILL**

*Objective:* To develop the hitter's bunting technique.

*Equipment Needed:* A crate of baseballs; a bat; two hats.

*Location:* Anywhere on the field.

*Description:* A hat should be placed near each baseline approximately ten feet apart. The batter assumes a good hitting stance. A feeder kneels approximately fifteen feet away from the batter to overhand toss the ball to the hitter. The hitter should pivot on his back leg as the feeder raises his arm to throw the ball. As the batter pivots, he should square his body to the feeder and slide his top hand down the bat to the midpoint of the barrel. The hitter should flex his knees as he gets into position to bunt the ball. To bunt the ball down the third-base line, the right-handed hitter should pull his left hand to his navel. To bunt the ball down the first-base line, the right-handed hitter should push his left hand away from his navel.

*Coaching Points:*

- The batter should catch the ball with his bat, rather than punch at the ball.
- The batter should never bunt the ball to the feeder.
- The batter should practice bunting with only his top hand on the bat, so that he can learn how to catch the ball with the barrel of his bat.
- The batter should never drop the head of the bat below his hands when bunting. Rather, he should bend his knees to bunt a low pitch.

**Drill #74: Bunting Drill. *Emphasis point: The hitter should slide his hand down the barrel of the bat and pivot on his back foot.***

## DRILL #75: OPPOSITE ANGLE DRILL

*Objective:* To develop the hitter's ability to hit the baseball to the opposite field.

*Equipment Needed:* A protective screen; a crate of baseballs; a bat.

*Location:* The baseball field.

*Description:* The hitter assumes a good stance at home plate. The protective screen is placed slightly to the base-line side. Against a right-handed hitter, the screen is placed slightly to the first-base line. Against a left-handed hitter, the screen is placed slightly to the third-base line. The hitter should assume his normal stance—facing the pitching mound. The pitcher should throw from a distance of forty feet away from home plate and aim for the outside two-thirds of the plate. The hitter should wait for the ball to enter the hitting zone, and then hit the ball to the opposite field.

*Coaching Points:*

- Once the player has demonstrated a basic mastery in hitting the ball to the opposite field, cones can be placed in the outfield gaps, and the batter can be required to hit the ball between the cones.
- If the ball is thrown to the inside of the plate, the batter should hit to his pull-side field.
- Once the player has demonstrated a basic mastery of waiting for the pitch to break into the hitting zone, the coach should use a T ball—or a similar-sized ball—to force the player to wait for an outside pitch.

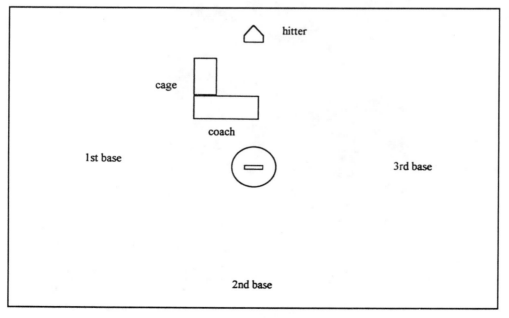

**Drill #75: Opposite Angle Drill.**

## DRILL #76: SELF TOSS WITH BOUNCE DRILL

*Objective:* To develop the hitter's weight shift control; to enable the hitter to feel the "load position" weight on the back half of his body.

*Equipment Needed:* A crate of tennis balls; a bat.

*Location:* The batting cage.

*Description:* The hitter holds a tennis ball with his bottom hand while he holds the bat with his top hand. Turning to the side from which he hits, the hitter bounces the ball approximately two feet in front of him. He should then step into the ball by crossing over with his back foot. His crossover step with the back foot should be followed by a step with his front foot. The front foot steps forward to get his body into the hitting position. His weight should be kept on his back leg. The player should then swing at the ball when it enters his hitting zone.

*Coaching Point:*

- This drill is designed to help the hitter feel the "load position."
- The proper techniques for swinging should be emphasized at all times.

**Drill #76: Self Toss with Bounce Drill.** *Emphasis point: The hitter should complete the step across and should be ready to hit the tennis ball.*

## DRILL #77: BASEBALL GOLF DRILL

*Objective:* To improve the hitter's bat control.

*Equipment Needed:* A bat; one ball.

*Location:* A baseball field.

*Description:* The hitter designates an object on the field as the "cup." He begins the drill by tossing the ball to himself in the manner of a fungo drill and hitting the ball towards the cup. The hitter should then proceed to the spot where the ball hits the ground and continue to toss and hit until he reaches the cup. After he completes one "hole," the player should pick out another object to be the cup and continue to play.

*Coaching Points:*

- The cup can be a foul pole, a base, etc.
- Variety can be added to this drill by conducting competition between players (i.e., fewest number of swings to complete the "course").

## DRILL #78: LINE DRIVE DRILL

*Objective:* To improve the hitter's hand-eye coordination.

*Equipment Needed:* A bat; a crate of baseballs; a protective screen.

*Location:* A batting cage.

*Description:* A feeder sits on a chair behind the screen in the batting cage and pitches to a batter. Strictly adhering the proper hitting technique, the batter should attempt to hit a line drive. If the batter pops up or hits a ground ball (instead of a line drive), the players switch roles.

*Coaching Point:*

- To increase the level of excitement level of the drill, the players can be divided into teams and score kept during this drill. For example, the players may play a designated number of innings. A fly ball or a ground ball is an out, while a line drive is a single. Each team gets three outs per inning. All runs must be forced in.

## DRILL #79: FUNGO DRILL

*Objective:* To improve the hitter's bat control.

*Equipment Needed:* A fungo bat; a crate of baseballs.

*Location:* A home plate.

*Description:* The hitter should stand on the grass along the baseline near home plate. He should then toss the ball to himself and attempt to hit the ball to a designated infielder. This drill is designed to improve the player's bat control by forcing him to hit line drives and ground balls to a specific location. If a fungo bat is not available, the drill may be done with a regulation bat.

*Coaching Point:*

- Once the player has mastered the basic mechanics of the fungo drill, he should be able to hit line drives, as well as one- and two-hoppers to a specific location, on command.

## DRILL #80: TOP AND BOTTOM DRILL

*Objective:* To improve the hitter's concentration and bat control.

*Equipment Needed:* A bat; a crate of baseballs.

*Location:* A batting cage; a soft toss screen.

*Description:* Holding two baseballs—one on top of the other—a feeder sits on a crate positioned a safe distance to one side of the batter. The feeder tosses both of the balls toward the hitter. The feeder should toss the balls to each of the three hitting zones. The feeder cues the batter to hit one of the two balls by saying "top" or "bottom" as he tosses the balls. The batter should hit the ball that has been designated by the feeder.

*Coaching Points:*

- The feeder should toss the balls slowly.
- The feeder may kneel on the ground if a crate is not available.

**Drill #80: Top and Bottom Drill.** *Emphasis point: The feeder should toss two balls to the batter and tell him which one to hit.*

## DRILL #81: ROPE DRILL

*Objective:* To teach the hitter to stay back and maintain balance on his back leg in order to avoid shifting his weight forward during his swing.

*Equipment Needed:* A rope or cord; a bat; a crate of baseballs.

*Location:* Batting cage.

*Description:* The rope should be tied around the hitter's waist. A player stands approximately 15 feet behind the hitter and holds the rope from an angle. Holding the rope from an angle keeps the rope-holder safe from being hit by the bat or foul ball. As the hitter assumes his stance, the rope-holder should pull the rope taut. The hitter should take some practice swings in order to feel the effect of the rope. A third player acts as a feeder and tosses the ball to the hitter as the hitter takes a normal cut. The rope-holder should not pull backwards on the rope. Rather, he should maintain the tension on the rope. If the hitter moves forward to hit the ball, the rope will restrain him. Having the rope restrain the hitter enables the batter to determine if he is lunging forward to hit the ball (which is a hitting technique flaw).

*Coaching Points:*

- It is important that the rope-holder position himself at a safe distance from the hitter.
- The hitter should keep his weight over his back leg as he swings the bat.

# CHAPTER 5

# PITCHING DRILLS

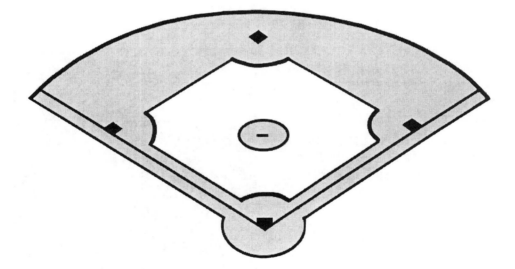

### DRILL #82: BALANCE AND POSITION DRILL

*Objective:* To improve the pitcher's balance when he is pitching from a windup.

*Equipment Needed:* A baseball; a glove.

*Location:* A bullpen.

*Description:* The drill begins by having a right-handed pitcher take a small step backward (approximately 12 inches) with his left foot. The step should be made at a 45-degree angle. He should subsequently lift his front leg to the point where his thigh is at a 90-degree angle from the ground. Once he obtains this position he should hold the spot for a predetermined amount of time. The acceptable amount of time ranges from three to ten seconds. Beginning pitchers should hold the position for ten seconds. As the pitcher becomes stronger and more skilled at maintaining his balance, the time a pitcher should hold his position should be shortened.

*Coaching Points:*

- This drill is the first of a series of four drills that should be mastered in sequence. Accordingly, the pitcher should master Drill #82 before he attempts Drill #83, etc.

- The pitcher should concentrate on lifting his lead knee to the balance position. He should not kick his leg out.

- The pitcher demonstrates mastery of the drill when he is able to lift his leg and hold the position without wobbling or falling.

- The pitcher will be able to maintain his balance more effectively if he keeps his shoulders and back slightly bowed—over his center of gravity.

**Drill #82: Balance and Position Drill.**
*Emphasis point: The pitcher's head should be directed at the target, his back should be straight, and his knee should be lifted straight up.*

## DRILL #83: BREAKING THE HANDS DRILL

*Objective:* To teach the pitcher the correct technique of a pitcher breaking his hands from the balance position.

*Equipment Needed:* A baseball; a glove.

*Location:* Bullpen.

*Description:* Balancing on his back leg, the pitcher holds his hands together as if he were praying. His elbows should point downward, as his forearms form an upside-down letter "V." As he moves from the "V" position, the pitcher should break his thumbs down to his thighs. The fingers of his back hand should point to the sky. The lead forearm should be at the same height as the lead shoulder (i.e., parallel to the ground). The back elbow should be at the same height as the back shoulder with the fingers of the throwing hand on top of the ball. At this moment, the ball should be facing in a direction opposite the pitcher's target (i.e., second base rather than home plate). The pitcher should freeze in this position.

*Coaching Points:*

- When the pitcher snaps his lead forearm out at the same height of his lead shoulder, he should visualize using his forearm to give someone a shove.

- The pitcher should not "throw" his hands away from his body. Such an action would cause him to lose his balance.

- An imaginary line should dissect the pitcher's back elbow, shoulders, and lead elbow. This line should lead straight to the target.

**Drill #83: Breaking the Hands Drill.**
***Emphasis point: As his knee goes down the pitcher should break his thumbs to his thigh, and should point the fingers of his back hand to the sky.***

## DRILL #84: KARATE KICK DRILL

*Objective:* To improve the pitcher's ability to keep his body closed throughout his pitching delivery.

*Equipment Needed:* None.

*Location:* Left field or right field foul lines.

*Description:* The drill involves the pitcher striding to the plate by performing a sharp-kick step with his lead leg from the balanced position that was discussed in Drill #80. He should kick sharply with his heel toward home plate. His kick should not be toward the third base line; rather, it should be toward home plate. The pitcher should land with his stance closed. Having a closed stance involves having his lead foot hit the turf at a 45-degree angle to the target. If the home plate is at 12:00, the lead foot should land on the turf pointing at 1:00. The more the foot opens toward the plate, the greater disadvantage the pitcher suffers. Maintaining a closed stance when the lead foot hits the ground enhances the pitcher's ability to throw the ball with high velocity.

*Coaching Point:*

- An imaginary straight line should run from a pitcher's back elbow through his shoulders and lead elbow to the target. This scenario is called "staying on line to the target."

**Drill #84: Karate Kick Drill.**
*Emphasis point: The pitcher's head should be on line to the target, with the back of his heel kicking straight to the target.*

## DRILL #85: TOWEL DRILL

*Objective:* To teach the pitcher to follow through on his delivery.

*Equipment Needed:* A towel; a chair.

*Location:* Anywhere on the field.

*Description:* The pitcher holds a hand towel in his throwing hand. He should grip the towel so that the towel is between his thumb and three fingers. His index finger, middle finger, and ring finger should be on the top of the towel. His pinky finger should be curled at the side of the hand, under the towel. Beginning from the loaded throwing position, the pitcher should simulate throwing the ball. To simulate throwing the ball, the pitcher should pop the towel across the seat of the chair. The pitcher should finish so that his back is parallel to the ground. His head should be level, with his chin parallel to the seat of the chair.

*Coaching Points:*

- The pitcher should keep his front shoulder closed as long as possible.
- The pitcher should follow through with a hip roll and with his the cleats of his back foot pointing to the sky.
- It is extremely important that the pitcher whip the towel. He should visualize his forearm and fingers acting as part of the whip, as he pops the towel across the seat of the chair.

## DRILL #86: ON LINE DRILL

*Objective:* To develop the pitcher's mechanics in sequence.

*Equipment Needed:* A baseball glove; a baseball.

*Location:* Left field or right field foul lines.

*Description:* The pitchers line up on the foul line and simulate pitching from a wind up. The coach should emphasize the mechanics that were described in drills 82-85. The foul line should be used as a guide to judge if the pitcher is staying on line. The foul line should extend through the middle of the pitcher's feet after he lands from a simulated pitch. The coach should check for correct pitching mechanics by commanding the pitchers to "pause" at various stages of their delivery.

*Coaching Points:*

- The coach may opt to not make a pause call so that the pitcher stays fluid during the drill.
- Repetition in practice is designed to create muscle memory. All factors considered, a pitcher should not think about his mechanics when actually pitching in a game.

**DRILL #87: ONE-KNEE DRILL**

*Objective:* To improve the pitcher's upper body mechanics.

*Equipment Needed:* A baseball glove; a baseball.

*Location:* Anywhere on the field.

*Description:* The pitchers are paired together. The right-handed pitchers should be instructed to kneel on their right knee. The left-handed pitchers should be instructed to kneel on their left knee. The pitchers should position their right knee at a 90-degree angle to the target. Their lead foot should be positioned at a 45-degree angle, keeping the hips closed. Their hands should be in the set position, forming an upside down "V." The pitcher should break his hands to the throwing position exactly as described in Drill #83. A straight line should run through the pitcher's stance from his back foot to the middle of his lead foot. The pitcher's upper body should finish flat against his lead leg.

*Coaching Points:*

- The pitcher should keep his lead shoulder and elbow closed as long as possible in the delivery.
- The pitcher should not pull his lead shoulder open. Such an action would cause his causes the delivery to be rushed, resulting in a pitch that is thrown too high.
- The pitcher should keep his lead side erect to improve deception by hiding the ball.
- The pitcher should keep his head on target (refer to Drill #85—Towel Drill).

**Drill #87: One-Knee Drill.** *Emphasis point: The pitcher's front leg should be lined up with his back knee; the pitcher should follow through with the hand on the opposite side of his lead leg.*

## DRILL #88: FACE THE WALL DRILL

*Objective:* To improve the pitcher's balance and ability to stay on line.

*Equipment Needed:* None.

*Location:* Anywhere near a wall.

*Description:* Facing the wall, the pitcher lifts his lead leg to a right angle. This action puts him in the balanced position. He should be positioned near the wall so that the wall prevents him from kicking out his lead leg toward the wall. The pitcher should use a karate kick from the balanced position (refer to Drill #84—Karate Kick Drill—for a description of a karate kick).

*Coaching Point:*

- If the pitcher kicks the wall, he is not doing the drill correctly.
- This drill is designed to train the pitcher to use the proper heel kick toward the plate. It is designed to teach him to refrain from kicking out toward the third-base foul line as he enters his delivery.
- The lead foot should dangle as the pitcher lifts his leg. He should keep his ankle loose as he moves though the pitching motion to karate kick to home plate.

**Drill #88: Face the Wall Drill. *Emphasis point: The pitcher should lift his lead leg should be straight up (if he kicks out, he'll kick the wall).***

## DRILL #89: BACK TO THE WALL DRILL

*Objective:* To improve the pitcher's balance and ability to stay on line.

*Equipment Needed:* None.

*Location:* Anywhere near a wall.

*Description:* With his back against the wall, the pitcher lifts his lead leg to a right angle. This action puts him in the balanced position by forcing him to keep his weight centered over his hips. The wall is also a helpful tool for teaching the pitcher to break his hands (refer to Drill #83 for a complete description of breaking the hands). The pitcher continues in his pitching motion as he stays parallel to the wall—pitching down the side of the wall.

*Coaching Point:*

- The wall forces the pitcher to keep his shoulders, elbows, and throwing hand in a straight line to the target.

**Drill #89: Back to the Wall Drill.** *Emphasis point: The pitcher should break the thumb on his throwing hand to the thigh up to the sky. If this is not done properly, his hand will hit the wall.*

### DRILL #90: WRIST DRILL

*Objective:* To isolate the pitching wrist and improve pitching velocity.

*Equipment Needed:* A baseball; a glove.

*Location:* Anywhere on the baseball field.

*Description:* The pitchers are paired off—approximately 20 feet apart. Each pitcher should kneel on one knee. Each pair of pitchers has a ball. The pitcher should hold his glove hand across his body. The pitcher with the ball should put the elbow of his throwing hand in his glove. He should throw the ball by snapping his wrist as his throwing elbow remains stationary.

*Coaching Points:*

- The pitcher should isolate his elbow with his glove hand and snap his wrist as fast as he can.
- The pitcher should snap his wrist through the center of the ball to increase the level velocity at which the ball is thrown.

**Drill #90: Wrist Drill. *Emphasis point: The pitcher should put the elbow of his throwing arm in his glove and use only his wrist to make sure his middle finger stays through the center of the baseball at the release.***

## DRILL #91: BALANCE BLOCK DRILL

*Objective:* To improve the pitcher's balance and develop his ability to throw with speed.

*Equipment Needed:* A balance block (a piece of wood approximately one-foot long and four-inches wide).

*Location:* Anywhere on the baseball field.

*Description:* The pitcher begins the drill with his lead foot at a 45-degree angle to the target. His lead foot is positioned on the balance block as he assumes the throwing position. He should then go through the pitching motion and hold his lead knee "rock solid," not allowing it to rotate forward or outward. If home plate is 12:00 o'clock, his toe should remain pointed at the 1:30 position. As he finishes his throwing motion, the pitcher should be balanced over his lead leg with a flat black. He should hold that position for an approximate count of three.

*Coaching Points:*

- The pitcher should keep his head on target, with his eyes focused straight ahead.
- The pitcher should keep his lead knee bent slightly.
- The pitcher's back heel should be pointed straight up to the sky when he sticks in the balanced position over his lead leg.

**Drill #91: Balance Block Drill.** *Emphasis point: The pitcher should be required to maintain his balance on the wooden block through his release while his chest is over his lead leg and his head is on target.*

## DRILL #92: WEIGHT SHIFT BOARD DRILL

*Objective:* To improve the pitcher's ability to keep his weight over his back leg.

*Equipment Needed:* A weight-shift board.

*Location:* Anywhere on the baseball field.

*Description:* The pitcher begins the drill on the weight-shift board. He may work from either a wind up or the stretch position. This drill is designed to help him keep his weight back as long as possible. If he shifts his weight forward too abruptly in this drill, the weight shift board will slam forward. The pitcher should use the karate kick technique from the balance position. He should exaggerate staying back on his back leg. The pitcher's hands and lead leg should break from the balance position at the same time. He should land softly on his lead leg as he shifts his weight.

*Coaching Points:*

- The weight shift board should not slam downward when the pitcher's front foot lands on the board.
- If the pitcher breaks his hands early, his pitching arm will be out in front of his body, and the ball will be pitched low.
- If the pitcher breaks his hands from his body late, his pitching arm will drag behind his body, and he will throw high.
- The pitcher should attempt to keep his head over his back foot as long as possible.

**Drill #92: Weight Shift Board Drill. *Emphasis point: The pitcher should keep his elbow parallel to the ground and his head on the target; he should maintain his weight on his back leg.***

## DRILL #93: CATCH THE BALL FROM THE PITCHING POSITION DRILL

*Objective:* To improve the pitcher's ability to keep his weight back and improve control.

*Equipment Needed:* A glove; a baseball.

*Location:* Anywhere on the baseball field.

*Description:* The pitcher begins the drill in the throwing position, balancing on his back leg. The coach tosses the ball to the pitcher. The pitcher should then complete his pitching motion.

*Coaching Points:*

- The pitcher should keep his back leg slightly bent.
- The pitcher should not be leaning or moving forward when the coach tosses the ball.
- The pitcher should have his weight centered over his hips.

**Drill #93: Catch the Ball From the Pitching Position Drill.** *Emphasis point:* *The pitcher should maintain balance on the back leg after his hands have broken hands; he should not drift forward until the ball is caught.*

## DRILL #94: STEP AND LIFT DRILL

*Objective:* To improve the pitcher's balance.

*Equipment Needed:* A baseball; a glove.

*Location:* A bullpen.

*Description:* The drill begins with the pitcher taking a small step back at a 45-degree angle. His angular step should be 12 inches or less. The pitcher should then lift his lead leg to the balance position.

*Coaching Points:*

- The pitcher should never swing or kick out his lead leg. Kicking out his lead leg will cause him to lose balance.
- The pitcher should point the toes of his lead foot down toward the ground. This action prevents him from kicking out his lead foot.
- Stepping back at a 45-degree angle increases a pitcher's level of balance because it decreases the rotation needed to get into the balance position by 45 degrees.

**Drill #94: Step and Lift Drill.** *Emphasis point: The pitcher should lift his leg until he is balanced, all the while keeping his eye on the target.*

## DRILL #95: PAINT THE CORNERS DRILL

*Objective:* To improve the pitcher's control by throwing all of his pitches at different spots on the carpet target.

*Equipment Needed:* A crate of baseballs; a glove; a carpet target.

*Location:* In front of the bullpen mound.

*Description:* After warming up for 10-15 minutes, the pitcher begins the drill by pitching "wave" fastballs to the outside corner of the carpet target. The carpet target should be hung on a fence approximately 50 feet from the pitcher. He should then work to the inside corner—again four to six inches off the plate. He should then go back to working at the outside corner, throwing one to three inches off the plate. He follows up by throwing at the inside corner, one to three inches off the plate. He should continue the same sequence of first pitching to the outside corner and then to the inside corner, aiming 4.25 inches within the strike zone.

*Coaching Points:*

- The pitcher should throw an equal number of pitches from the windup and stretch positions.

- This drill should be performed daily. The pitchers should throw approximately 50 feet away from the plate. Because the pitcher is not working from a mound, the pitcher's arm is not overly stressed in this drill. A typical workout involves somewhere between 20 and 40 pitches.

- Ideally, the pitcher should not move from one spot until he hits that spot. Coaches should closely monitor a pitcher's results in this drill, keeping in mind that a pitcher's accuracy may vary from day to day. As such, compensation should be made to accommodate the "bad" days a pitcher may suffer in his accuracy.

- Approximately four to six inches from the respective center of the "plate," the carpet is colored blue because it is the area in which a "wave" pitch is thrown. The batter should wave (i.e., miss the ball) when he swings. Approximately zero to three inches from the edge is colored black to signify the outside edge of the plate. Since the plate is 17 inches wide, the middle 8.5 inches is colored red, signifying fire (i.e., a pitcher will get burned if he pitches in the red area). The inner and outer 4.25 inches within the strike zone is colored green. Green signifies money. If a pitcher can consistently pitch in this area, he may go a long way and makes lots of money. A strike zone is both horizontal and vertical. The vertical strike zone is based on a 5'10" player. Any pitch between 28-48 inches is in the vertical red zone. To pitch "up" in the zone, a pitcher should throw the ball approximately 48-58 inches high.

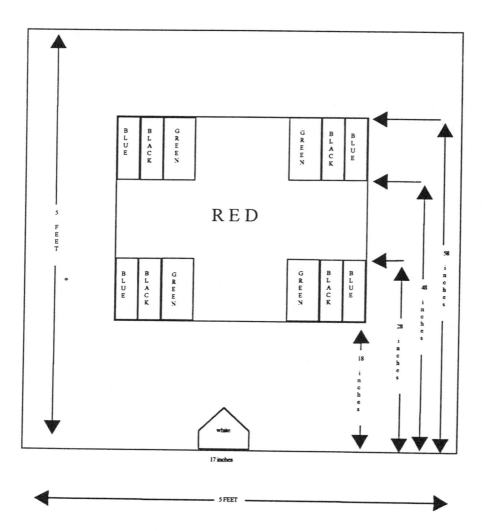

**Drill #95: Paint the Corners Drill.**

## DRILL #96: BULLPEN WORKOUT DRILL

*Objective:* To improve the pitcher's control.

*Equipment Needed:* A glove; several new baseballs; full catching gear for the catcher.

*Location:* A bullpen.

*Description:* The pitcher should warm-up by stretching, throwing, long-tossing, and sprinting before he begins this drill. The drill involves having the pitcher work from the mound and following the same routine described in Drill #95. The number of pitches thrown during a bullpen workout and the number of bullpen workouts during the week should vary with the role of the pitcher (i.e., his workout varies according to whether he is a starter, reliever, or a closer). A starter should complete this workout once a week; a reliever should complete the workout two times during the week; and a closer should complete this workout on a daily basis.

*Coaching Points:*

- During the preseason, the starting pitcher should work up to throwing 100 pitches.

- During the season, the starting pitcher should throw approximately 20 to 40 pitches a workout. He should increase the number of pitches if he is skipped in the rotation.

- A closer should throw only those types of pitches he will be required to throw in a game.

- The pitcher should get on the mound *every single day* with the exception of the day after a starting rotation. However, he should never throw full speed. He should throw $1/2$ to $3/4$ speed depending on the variants. Variants to consider in structuring a pitcher's bullpen workout include the number of pitches he threw in the previous game, the types of pitches (i.e., curve balls, fastballs, etc.) he threw, the number of days between games he pitched, etc.

## DRILL #97: BANANA ROUTE DRILL

*Objective:* To improve the pitcher's ability to cover first base on a ground ball hit to the right side of the infield.

*Equipment Needed:* A crate of baseballs; a fungo bat.

*Location:* An infield.

*Description:* The pitcher stands on the mound. The second baseman take his position at second, while the first baseman assumes his position at first base. The catcher also takes his position at home plate, as the coach stands nearby with a fungo bat and a ball in his hand. The drill begins by having the pitcher throw the ball to the catcher at home plate. The coach then hits fungo to the right side of the infield. The pitcher should respond to the hit ball by sprinting to the first-base foul line. He should take a banana-shaped route so that he is running parallel to the foul line on his way to first base. His banana route should allow him to run parallel to the foul line for approximately the last 20 feet of the base path. He should always sprint to the first-base foul line on any ground ball hit to the right side of the infield.

*Coaching Points:*

- On a slow roller, the pitcher will have less time. Accordingly, his banana route should be flatter when a slow roller is hit (i.e., he should run more directly toward the first base).

- The pitcher should always hit the inside of the first base bag with his right foot so that he can stay in fair territory and not interfere with the runner.

- The pitcher should not avoid fielding the ball. He should field any ball which he has an opportunity to field.

## DRILL #98: BUNT FIELDING DRILL

*Objective:* To improve the pitcher's ability to field the ball consistently.

*Equipment Needed:* A baseball; a bat.

*Location:* Infield.

*Description:* All the infielders take their positions. A hitter assumes his position at the plate. The drill begins by having the pitcher throw a strike to home plate which the hitter attempts to bunt. The pitcher then responds to the bunt by fielding the bunt. If the ball isn't rolling, the pitcher should field the ball off his outside foot. If the ball is rolling, the pitcher should field the ball as an infielder. An infielder should round the rolling ball and field it to the left of his belly button. The pitcher should always grab the ball with his whole hand—not just the fingers. He should point his lead shoulder to the target.

*Coaching Points:*

- A bunted ball that is not rolling should be fielded by a pitcher from the outside of his right foot. Fielding the ball in this manner puts the pitcher in the loaded position.

- The pitcher should use his whole hand to field the ball, pushing the ball down to the ground as he grasps it.

**Drill #98: Bunt Fielding Drill.** *Emphasis point: The pitcher should sprint to the ball and field the ball off his back foot to eliminate the need to step and patting their hands together (an unnecessary "habit" that some players do before throwing).*

## DRILL #99: PICKOFF CRATE DRILL

*Objective:* To improve the pitcher's pickoff move to first base.

*Equipment Needed:* A crate of baseballs for each pitcher.

*Location:* Right field foul line.

*Description:* The pitchers align along the right field line. Each pitcher places his crate from his position at an angle and distance comparable to the angle and distance between the mound and first base. The crate should be placed so that its open side is facing the pitcher. The pitcher should barely get off the ground as he brings the ball to his ear to throw. He should use the jump hop method, hopping in the air with both feet and squaring his feet off to the target—either the crate or first base. Using the crate as a teaching tool is designed to train the pitcher to keep his pickoff throw low.

*Coaching Points:*

- As the pitcher becomes skilled at the pickoff move to first base, he should vary his looks to first base.
- If a baserunner is stealing, the pitcher should take a slide-step as he delivers a pitch to first base. The slide-step is a technique in which the pitcher raises his lead leg only slightly off the ground a few inches and slides it across the ground.
- When slide-stepping, the pitcher should concentrate on staying with the slope of the mound and pointing his lead shoulder down. The slide-step facilitates a quick delivery to home plate, increasing the odds of the catcher throwing the runner out.

**Drill #99: Pickoff Crate Drill.**

## DRILL #100: (ONE-TWO-THREE) LEFTY PICKOFF DRILL

*Objective:* To improve a left-handed pitcher's pickoff move to first base.

*Equipment Needed:* A baseball.

*Location:* The infield.

*Description:* The drill involves a left-handed pitcher on the mound, a catcher, a first baseman and a baserunner on first. The coach assigns "#1" to the catcher, "#2" to the first baseman, and "#3" to the baserunner. As the pitcher assumes the stretch position, the coach tells the pitcher to look at "3" (i.e. the baserunner), and throw to "1" (i.e. the catcher). The coach should continue the drill by instructing the pitcher to look at various positions and to throw to a particular assigned number. For example, the coach's commands should be of the following nature: "look 1 - throw 2;" "look 2 - throw 1;" "look 3 - throw 2;" etc. Initially, the pitchers may have some difficulty remembering which player is what number. Over time, however, pitchers tend to pick up on the numbering system fairly quickly.

*Coaching Points:*

- Pitchers are creatures of habit. This drill is designed to force them to vary their routines and pitching patterns. All factors considered, the more variance in the pitcher's arsenal of pickoff moves, the more hesitant the baserunners will be.

- When attempting to pickoff a baserunner, a left-handed pitcher should step at 45-degree angle toward home plate. Stepping at a 45-degree angle will cause deception and make it relatively difficult for the baserunner to get a good jump toward second base.

**Drill #100: (One-Two-Three) Lefty Pickoff Drill.** *Emphasis point: The pitcher should take to balance step to his left at a 45-degree angle with his head at different points in order to trick the baserunner and should step completely off the mound after throwing to first base.*

## DRILL #101: PICKOFFS TO SECOND BASE

*Objective:* To prevent the baserunner from getting a good jump and stealing third base.

*Equipment Needed:* A baseball.

*Location:* The infield.

*Description:* This drill involves a pitcher on the mound and a shortstop, a second baseman and a catcher assuming their normal positions in the field. The pitcher has three pickoff moves to second available to him—the jump hop, the reverse jump hop, and the wrap move. The jump hop involves the pitcher hopping in the air off of both feet. During the jump hop move, the pitcher hops toward his throwing hand. The reverse jump hop also requires the pitcher to jump in the air off of both feet. However, during the reverse jump hop move, the pitcher hops toward his glove hand. The third pickoff move—the wrap move—requires the pitcher to lift his lead leg up and wrap it around his body in the direction of his throwing hand.

*Coaching Points:*

- A pitcher should be skilled in at least two of the three pickoff moves to second base.
- The pitcher should point his lead shoulder to second base as he completes his move.
- It is important for the pitcher to keep his weight centered over his hips. This action allows him to execute a quicker jump hop and gives him better balance.
- If the pitcher determines that the baserunner is stealing, he should use the slide-step technique to deliver the ball to the catcher (refer to Drill #99—Pickoff Crate Drill—for additional information on the slide-step technique).

Glenn Cecchini is the head baseball coach at Barbe High School in Lake Charles, Louisiana. Since 1988, Coach Cecchini's teams have enjoyed a .753% winning percentage and six district championships. For six consecutive years, his teams have been ranked nationally by *Collegiant Baseball Magazine*, *Baseball America Magazine*, and *USA Today.* A national winner of the 1997 Easton Master Coach Award, Coach Cecchini was named 5A State Coach of the Year in 1998 when his Barbe Bucs captured the 5A Louisiana State Championship.

Raissa Cecchini is Glenn Cecchini's lifelong partner and assistant baseball coach. A highly successful rodeo competitor and girl's basketball coach, Raissa chose to focus her coaching talents on helping her husband build a championship baseball program at Barbe High School. Like her husband Glenn, Raissa was named a national winner of the 1997 Easton Master Coach Award. With Raissa's influence, the Barbe Buc baseball program was raised from the level of just another high school baseball team to a national powerhouse.

Jeff Walker possesses a Master of Education degree from Schreiner College along with a Bachelor of Arts degree from Northeast Louisiana. A high school coach with over 14 years experience, Walker has contributed to numerous other projects for Coaches Choice. A past contributor to Scholastic Coach and Athletic Director magazine and the author of *Coaching Football's 40 Nickel Defense*, Walker resides in Kerrville, Texas with his family, Paula and Gabe Walker.

# ADDITIONAL BASEBALL RESOURCES FROM

## BOOKS

### *PITCHING FROM THE GROUND UP*
by Bob Bennett
1997 • 223 pp • Paper • ISBN 1-57167-076-9 • $20.00

### *DARE TO HIT .400*
by Jake Boss and Kevin Ziesman
1999 • 96 pp • Paper • ISBN 1-57167-362-8 • $14.95

## VIDEOS

### *CATCHING SKILLS AND DRILLS: VOLUME 1*
by Jerry Weinstein
1998 • Running Time: 73 min.
ISBN 1-57167-284-2 • $40.00

### *CATCHING SKILLS AND DRILLS: VOLUME 2*
by Jerry Weinstein
1998 • Running Time: 73 min.
ISBN 1-57167-285-0 • $40.00